Farmer Producer Organization (FPO)

Abouth the Authors

Prof. (Dr.) Sankar Kr Acharya, presently, Dean, Post Graduate Studies; former Head, Department of Agril Extension and Director, Extension Education, Bidhan Chandra Krishi Viswavidyalaya, Mohanpur, WB, born on 6th October, 1960, started his career as Assistant Professor at BCKV in 1988 and has been in teaching, research and extension over 35 years. An erudite teacher as well as an elegant speaker, is internationally acclaimed for his unique research domain of Social Entropy and Energy Metabolism, Social Ecology and Environmental Sociology, Enterprise Ecology Framework, Farm Stewardships: The Transition from Conservation, Technology Socialization Process, and The Social Ecology of Livelihood, which have got tremendous policy as well as scholastic importance. Research Publication: 247 in National and International Journals. Book Publication: 113 books authored / co-authored. Expert Member, Agriculture Commission; Marketing and Extension Sub Committee, Govt. of West Bengal; Expert member WWF projects in BTR (Buxa Tiger Reserve Project); Expert member; DFID project on Primary Education (DPEP); Rapid Environment Impact Analysis, Visited Italy, France, Germany, China , Sri Lanka and Bangladesh. Delivered 33 Key note addresses, 13, invited and lead speakers in International Congress, Chaired 19 Sessions in International conferences, and Editors of a score of national and international journals. He has so far been awarded with 15 best paper awards in National and International Conferences Organizing Secretary of two International Conferences, held in the years, 2016 & 2018, Jointly Organized by Department of Agricultural Extension, BCKV, WB and Krishisanskriti, New Delhi. He has also been honoured to be selected as the Convener of Panel (PE-32) entitled The hunger, poverty and silence, of IUAES, University of Manchester, UK, 2013 .Co-PI of ICAR, NAHEP and World Bank funded project on Conservation Agriculture. So, far he has successfully guided 19 Ph D scholars, of which one awarded with DAAD fellowship, Germany and two other placed as visiting scholars at Ohio State University and Cornel University, 2020-21, USA; 83 M Sc students from BCKV CU, KU, Vidyasagar University. He is the fellow of ISEE, IARI, New Delhi, Fellow , BIOVED, He is now acting as editor, reviewer of a good number of national and international journals. Fellow Award, ISEE(ICAR-IARI, New Delhi), 2019 Awards and Distinctions: Distinguish Scholar Award, Krishisanskriti, New Delhi; Certificate of Merit for standing First class first at M Sc(Ag) in Agricultural Extension, 1986; ;Honorary Appointment to the Research Board of Advisors, The American Biographic Institute (2003) ;He has been honored to be selected as the Convener of Panel (PE-32) entitled the hunger, poverty and silence, of World Congress, IUAES, University of Manchester, UK, 2013 ;He has been honored to be selected as the Convener of

Panel (P-102) entitled,' Uncertainties, Unpredictability and Marginalization: The impact and mitigation for survival of agriculture and humanity, of the 19th World Congress, IUAES-WAU, 14-20 October, 2023, New Delhi, India, 2023 ;Honored to be nominated as Expert Member, Working group on Agricultural Extension and Training, West Bengal State Agriculture Commission (2007) ;Honored to be nominated by the Hon'ble Vice-Chancellor, BCKV to Act as an Expert Member, DPEP, A DFID, UK, project for planning and revamping primary education through POA of GOVT of India.(1995) Expert Member, Buxa Tiger Reserve Project funded by WWF(World Wide Wild Life Funding), 1998 ; Dr Daulat Singh Memorial Award, Society of Extension Education, Distinguished Professor and Academician Award, Research Education Solution (RES), M S Swaminathan School of Agriculture, Centurion University(2022); Diamond Achievers Award, Council for Academic Performance and Appraisal, New Delhi(2022) ;Honorary Fellowship Award, BIOVED Research Institute of Agriculture and Technology, Allahabad on Occasion of Agricultural Scientists and Farmers' Congress. Achievers of German patent (Utility model no.20202310273) :Novel LOT based inventory management system with radio controlled pallet racking for storage solution. Fellow, West Bengal Academy of Science and Technology(WAST)

Mr. Saumyesh Acharya is currently pursuing Ph.D. in Agricultural Extension at Visva-Bharati (A Central University), Santiniketan and has been outstanding in his academics as well as in the research arena. He has qualified in both UGC NET 2022 in Adult Education/ Continuing Education/ Andragogy/ Non-Formal Education, and also ASRB NET 2023 in Agricultural Extension. His outstanding research works have been published in term of five research papers as the main author and four research papers as co-author in nationally reputed journals (NAAS Rating ranging from 5.13 to 5.95). Besides, he has presented nine papers in the International/ National level Seminar/ Conference/ Congress, abstracts/ extended summary of which have also been published. He has been conferred the prestigious Ganga Singh Chahuan Memorial Award for his extraordinary contribution in Extension Education by Society of Extension Education, Agra. He has also contributed two book chapters to IEEC-BHU. His M.Sc. Dissertation work has been recognized by the Indian Society of Extension Education (ISEE, New Delhi) in the form of the Best Oral Paper Presentation Award at ISEE National Seminar 2023 organized in UAS, Bangalore. He has also received another two oral paper presentation awards in two International Conferences. He has participated in a Summer School on "Emerging Research Techniques for Sustainable Agriculture and Natural Resource Management". He has been advancing his post-graduate research on Farmer Producers Organisation (FPOs) in his Doctoral research.

Dr Tapan Kr Mandal, born in 1962, is now working as Associate Professor, Department of Agriculture Extension, Bidhan Chandra Krishi Viswavidyalaya, Mohanpur.As a CSIR fellow, he proved his mettle in Ph D research and subsequently as a faculty in the genre of extension science, he has up scaled himself to become an erudite teacher and researcher par excellence . So far , he has published 40 research papers and authored good no. Of books and book chapters. He has successfully guided 4 Ph D scholars and a good number of PG students.

Farmer Producer Organization (FPO) The Neo-institutional Revolution in Indian Farming

Sankar Kr Acharya
Saumyesh Acharya
Tapan K Mandal

FU 75, Pitam Pura
New Delhi 110034
publishmywork23@gmail.com
Mob. 91-8447075807

Print ISBN: 978-93-61342-62-2

ebook ISBN: 978-93-61341-32-8

Preface

Albeit we achieve green revolution, we had a quantum jump of food grain production from 50 million tons to 130 million tons during seventies to set the nation free from begging bowl syndromes, yet a plethora of issues remained unsolved. Disruption of ecology and poor status of farm income which has been small, uncertain and frivolous needs to be redressed with utmost care and highest priority. Today's farmers need happy return which will be enough to meet basic minimum, secured and hassle free. So, they desperately need a company status of their own to showcase their product and harvest the happy return. Farmer Producer Organization (FPO) is one of the greatest institutional innovation for the much needed transformation of subsistence farming into entrepreneurial farming in India. The FPOs provides dream, desire and destiny of the farmers on field or in their family, in the state or national level. They are the instrument of fulfilling their dreams, executing their desire into actions and making agriculture a dependable means to survive and to win. Whenever the government system started witnessing institutional confinement and formalities, the FPOs are opening up a new front of public-private partnership, entrepreneurial innovations, business ecosystem, branding and socializing the commercial dent of agriculture in a redefined and renewed manner. The book, Farmer Producer Organization (FPO): The Neo-institutional Revolution in Indian Farming, has become a phenomenal scholastic stride at a time when Indian farming needs a true entrepreneurial revolution for both up scaling and upskilling the plight of farmers

Authors

Contents

1

Introduction

Albeit a mammoth volume of food grain production in India, 320 million tons and close to 350 million tons of vegetables production in 2023 evinces the emergence of mighty Indian agriculture over the geo-political expanse at global level, yet the income from agriculture to her 140 millions of farmers is not secured, persistent and satisfying. This is due to a mal orchestration of weather-market-job-technolgy uncertainties. The farmers producer organization offers them a new hope and aspiration for small-marginal tiny agricultural producers of India.

Farmer Producer Organization (FPO) is one of the greatest institutional innovation for the much needed transformation of subsistence farming into entrepreneurial farming in India. The FPOs provides dream, desire and destiny of the farmers on field or in their family, in the state or national level. They are the instrument of fulfilling their dreams, executing their desire into actions and making agriculture a dependable means to survive and to win. Whenever the government system started witnessing institutional confinement and formalities, the FPOs are opening up a new front of public-private partnership, entrepreneurial innovations, business strategies, branding and socializing the commercial dent of agriculture in a redefined and renewed manner.

FPO opens the corridor wherein Government agencies, officials, common farmers, poor and rich, male and female, are equally participating in the process through a collective wisdom, information sharing and enterprise innovations. FPO helps reduce risk, improves new corridors for entrepreneurship and a new institutional expanse for redefining the value of agriculture for 21st century.

The crucial issues for the successful functioning of FPOs are related to general awareness among FPO functioning in terms of

(i) company laws, financial norms, regulatory process and supply chain management.

(ii) the fund flow mechanism or credit flow into the FPOs has become complex due to the procedural inadequacy or integracies .

(iii) market- linked extension is yet to make FPOs a prudential way of doing agribusiness both in quantum and quality.

(iv) FPO products have to compete with, today or tomorrow with the gigantic corporate sectors, national or multi-nationals. So, how to go for co-integrating small FPOs into a competitive capability also needs a focused attention.

The success of India's agriculture and the the glorious survival of Indian farmers depend on how best and how faster the farmers can adapt to the new age agribusiness scenario. We have to take it in our mind that farmers are doing agriculture just not to feed their family and nation, but also they are doing with entrepreneurship to generate happy returns for a glorious life to lead. Albeit FPO is at its growing stage, it can offer the most dependable way to escalate the income and ensure the livelihood with both grace and glory. The present research has been empirically tested and theorized in Odhisha with the following objectives.

Objectives

a) To estimate the level of entrepreneurial behavior of farmers in FPO in terms of (i) Net return (ii) Marketable surpl (iii) Brandin iv) Entrepreneurial communication

b) To estimate these 4 predicted characteristics of the enterprising farmers under FPO in terms of a set of socio-economic and managerial variables.

c) To estimate the inter and intra level of interaction between sets of predicted and predictor variables as accommodated in the study.

d) To generate policy at micro-level for farmers upskilling and upgradation of the entrepreneurial behavior of study.

e) To go for SWOT analysis of both farmers and FPOs to isolate the stronger and weaker points of enterprise ecology under study.

2

Neo-institutional Revolution and Farmer Producer Organization (FPO)

To tackle modern-day challenges and attain a sustainable growth while managing farm enterprises, the farmers have to undergo rigorous behavioral change to transform themselves as entrepreneur. Thus, the present chapter deals with incorporating an understanding about the idea of an entrepreneur and entrepreneurship and the organization level, present status and promotional opportunities of FPOs.

2.1 Who is an Entrepreneur?

An entrepreneur is someone or a group of individuals who conceptualize, start, and sustain for a long enough period of time a social organization that provides financial rewards, or, to put it another way, who see a business opportunity and create a firm to pursue it. (Cole,1968)

The entrepreneur has a deep interest in practical and technological issues and is a creative problem-solver. However, rather than utilizing especially novel strategies, the majority of entrepreneurial operations include adjusting to the way company is conducted and combining inputs that are strikingly similar to those combinations currently in use. (Hagen,1962)

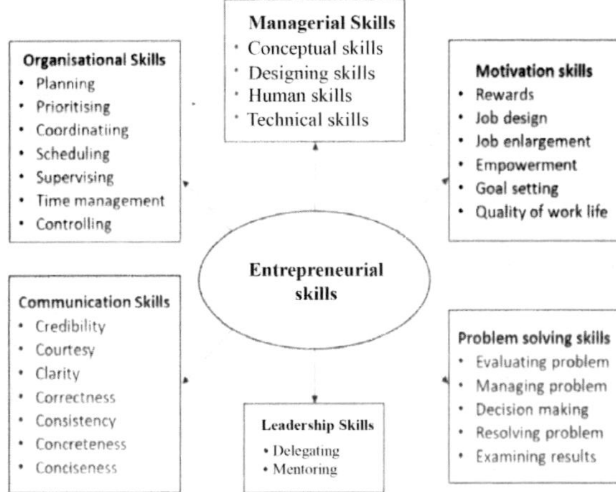

Fig. 2.1: Skills of an entrepreneur

2.2 Concept of Entrepreneurship

Entrepreneurship is also the process of creating, launching, and managing a new firm, which is usually a small one at first.Entrepreneurship is the ability and willingness to plan, organise, and run a business enterprise, taking on any risks necessary to do so, with the goal of making a profit. It is also the method by which a person or group of people locates a business opportunity, acquires the resources essential for its exploitation, and uses those resources.

Entrepreneurship research dates back to the late 17th and early 18th centuries, to the work of Richard Cantillon and Adam Smith. However, until a significant comeback in business and economics from the late 1970s, entrepreneurship was mostly neglected experimentally and theoretically. This neglect peaked in the late 19th and early 20th centuries. In the 20th century, Joseph Schumpeter's work in the 1930s, together with that of prominent Austrian economists Carl Menger, Ludwig von Mises, and Friedrich von Hayek, played a significant role in the understanding of entrepreneurship.

"An entrepreneur is a person who is willing and able to convert a new idea or invention into a successful innovation," says Schumpeter. The assumption that entrepreneurship leads to economic growth is an interpretation of the residual in endogenous growth theory, and it is hotly debated in academic economics as such. Thus, entrepreneurshipis:

(i) A function of group level pattern.

(ii) A function of managerial skill and leadership.

(iii) An organisational building function.

(iv) A function of high achievement.

(v) Input-completing and gap filling.

(vi) Afunction of status withdrawal function.

(vii) A functionof social, political and economic structure

(Schumpeter,1970)

Entrepreneurship in social organization is a highly complex process. It is the result of the interaction of various characteristics such as natural endowments, historical traditions, educational and cultural standards, social stratification, religious and moral values, and the development of family organizations over time.

(Bhatt, 1974)

Entrepreneurship can be defined as a creative and innovative response to the environment. Such a reaction can occur in any field of social endeavor—business, industry, agriculture, education, social work, and so on. Being new or doing things that are already done in a new way is thus a simple definition of entrepreneurship. Entrepreneurship is also a collection of entrepreneurial personality traits.(Rao and Mehta,1978)

2.3 Concept of Entrepreneurial Behaviour

Behaviour is an individual's response to stimuli and includes what he knows (knowledge), what he can do (skill), both mental and physical, what he thinks (attitude), and what he actually does (action). (Leagans,1961)

Behaviour is a function of many personal factors, such as motives, habits, attitudes, and so on, as well as many environmental factors, such as norms, laws, rewards, and punishments(Calder and Ross,1976)

Behaviour is a function of a continuous process of multi-directional interaction between the person and the situations, including other people, that he or she encounters (Fisher,1982).

Entrepreneurial behaviour is the result of an interaction of individual, situational, psychological, social, and experiential factors. (Rao,1985)

Singh (1986), stated that entrepreneurial behaviour (EB) was a function of anindividual's personality characteristics and environmental factors. This could berepresentedas

EB=f(PE); where,

P=Personality characteristics

E=Environmental factors

Entrepreneurial behaviour is the change in knowledge, skill, and attitude of entrepreneurs toward the chosen enterprise.(Manjula,1995),

Entrepreneurial behaviour is defined as an individual's decision to pursue a specific business in order to profit. (Patel and Sanoria,1997),

The causal sequences of entrepreneurial behaviour: Ideological values - Family socialisation - Achievement drive - E.B. (Mc Clelland, 1965),

Entrepreneurial Behaviour involves

(i) **Information Seeking:** Here, the entrepreneur becomes curious and seeks more and more information in order to launch a new business/venture.

(ii) **Information Processing:** The entrepreneur will then process the information gathered and create a database that will be useful in running the business.

(iii) **Information Disseminating:** Following information processing, the accumulated information is disseminated to external sources, which will benefit the business and new initiatives.

2.4 Dimensions of Entrepreneurial Behaviour

Fraser (1961) investigated small line entrepreneurs in a rural village in Orissa and discovered that people with high need achievement demonstrated more entrepreneurial spirit and less involvement in traditional soil cultivation than those with low n-Ach.

Achievement motivation as an individual's need or desire to perform or do better not so much for the sake of social recognition or prestige as it is to achieve an inner sense of personal accomplishment and proposed a model of achievement motivation known as the A-T-D model. In summary, an increase in the level of n-Ach (A) in society is associated with an increase in the rate of development (D) with a time lag (T) that is always positive. (Mc Clelland,1961)

Achievement motivation was defined by Neill and Rogers (1963) as the value instilled in an individual through a sociological process in which the individual feels a need or desire to excel in reaching certain goals solely for the satisfaction of reaching the goal and not for the rewards of the goals or ends involved. Farmer achievement motivation leads to individual farming excellence. They discovered a significant relationship between the need for achievement of Ohio state farmers (U.S.A.) and some indicators of farming excellence such as production man work units, man days of labour on the farm, and the number of acres in the farm.

The characteristics/dimensions of entrepreneurs are as follows: need achievement; desire for responsibility; preference for moderate risk; perception of probability of risk; stimulation by feedback; energetic activity; future oriented; skill in organizing and attitude towards money. (Mc Clelland,1969)

De (1986) discovered that socioeconomic status, education, knowledge of HYV of wheat practises, information sources used, innovative orientation, and progressive values had a positive and significant relationship with entrepreneur characteristics farmers.

The transitioning from family management to enterprise management may be easier than transitioning from paid employment to self-employment. (Harper and Vyakaranam,1988)

Swamy (1988) concluded that farmers were the most innovative and entrepreneurial, migrating early by identifying income-generating opportunities outside the village and providing information for their success.

2.5. Entrepreneurial Process

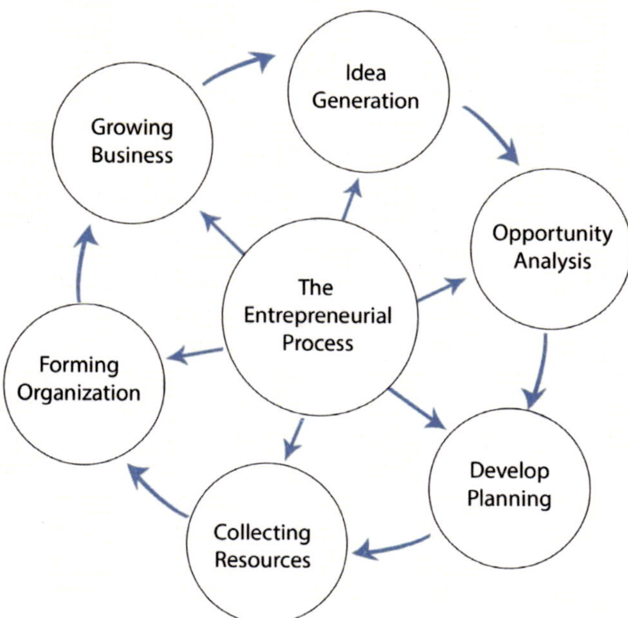

Fig. 2.2: Entrepreneurial Process [Source:Parsadi (Fahad Usmani, Jan 31,2022)]

2.5.1 Idea Generation

This is the first step in starting a business. An idea can be both a problem and a solution. Here, the entrepreneur identified a viable business opportunity. The feasibility study will be conducted by the entrepreneur, with input from other stakeholders.

2.5.2 Opportunity Analysis

The entrepreneur will evaluate the opportunity after identifying it. They will examine whether the opportunity adds value to the business or the consumer, whether it is long-term sustainable if the profit is healthy, market competition, the risks associated with the opportunity, and whether the entrepreneur's product or service is different or better than the competition.

The following questions should be addressed by the entrepreneur:

Is it worthwhile to invest capital, resources, and energy in this opportunity?

Can we do better?

2.5.3 Developing Plan

After analyzing the opportunity, the entrepreneur creates a plan to capitalise on it and launch the business. This is an important stage in the entrepreneurial process. The plan will include a business strategy and operating structures, as well as steps for forming the company. It will include information about the company's objectives, goals, mission statement, and products or services.

2.5.4 Collecting Resources

A new business requires resources such as financing, human labour, materials, and so on. Self-financing is an option for entrepreneurs who are self-sufficient. They may, however, seek funds from investors or financial institutions.

Entrepreneurs now have a new option known as crowdfunding. Entrepreneurs use these platforms to raise awareness about their businesses and solicit support. Businesses can quickly raise a significant amount if the idea resonates with the audience.

2.5.5 Forming Organization

Once the entrepreneur has secured the necessary funds and resources, the company will be launched and a legal entity will be formed. The organization's structure will be determined by its needs.

The entrepreneur will name the business and file the necessary paperwork with the government to establish an LLC, WLL or PLC, Corporation, or Non-profit.

2.5.6 Growing Business

After the company is established, it will begin producing goods or providing services. The entrepreneur will ensure that the company runs smoothly and grows. The operating plan will now be carried out. The entrepreneur will receive regular status updates and will compare actual and planned progress. If things don't go as planned, they will take corrective actions to bring the progress on track.

2.6 Entrepreneurship: The DynamicNeed

Entrepreneur is a business leader who has a pivotal role in fostering economic growth. Entrepreneurship helps solving the following problems:

- Employment Generation.
- National Production.
- Dispersal of Economic power.
- Balance Regional development (Satish Tanuja and Dr. S.L. Gupta, 1999)

2.7 New Concept of Entrepreneurs

Following the implementation of financial reforms and the opening up of the economy, the term entrepreneur has been defined as the one who detects, identifies, and evaluates a new situation in his environment and directs the necessary economic system adjustment. He is the person who envisions an industrial enterprise for a specific purpose, takes initiative, takes risks, is determined to see his project through to completion, and in the process, performs one or more of the perceived opportunities, for profitable investments, explores the prospects of starting manufacturing, and obtains necessary industrial licences, etc. (Vasant Desai,1999)

2.8 Conceptual Framework of Entrepreneurship

Entrepreneurship "entails collaborating to initiate changes in production." Entrepreneurship is a cyclical phenomenon that appears and then disappears until it reappears to initiate another change. Wilken classifies changes into five categories:

(*i*) Initial Expansion.

(*ii*) Subsequent Expansion.

(*iii*) Factor Innovations.

(*iv*) Production Innovations.

(*v*) Market Innovations (Prashad Awadesh,1988)

2.9 Farmer Producer Organization(FPO)

FPO is a farmer-led organisation that works for, with, and for farmers. It is a means of bringing small and marginal farmers, as well as other small producers, together to form their own business enterprise, which will be managed by professionals. FPO enable small farmers to participate more effectively in the market, thereby increasing agricultural production, productivity, and profitability. (Shubhangi, 2016). It has emergedasone of the most effective pathwaystoaddressmany challenges of agriculture, specifically improved access to investments, technology, inputs and markets (DAC, 2013).

The primary goal of FPO is to increase producer income through their own organisation. Small producers do not have the volume (both inputs and output) to benefit from economies of scale. Furthermore, in agricultural marketing, there is a long chain of intermediaries who frequently work in a non-transparent manner, resulting in a situation in which the producer receives only a small portion of the value that the ultimate consumer pays. Primary producers can benefit from economies of scale through aggregation. They will also have more bargaining power than bulk produce buyers and bulk input suppliers. (NABARD, 2015). It is widely acknowledged that commercialization of small-scale, resource-poor farmers' produce is closely related to higher productivity, greater specialisation, and higher income. (Bernard and Spielman,2009).

FPOs enable small farmers to reduce transaction costs associated with obtaining inputs and outputs as well as market information (Stockbridge et al., 2003). Other significant benefits of establishing FPO include the creation of countervailing power, favourable access to capital markets, risk management, and income increases. (Datta, 2004).

2.10 Benefits of FPO

1. The cost of production or cultivation may be decreased by purchasing all essential materials in bulk at wholesale rates, as well as using specialised farm equipment hiring services.

2. Aggregation of product and bulk transportation minimise marketing costs, hence improving profitability and the net value realised by the producer.
3. Building scale through commodity aggregation takes advantage of economies of scale, size, attracting merchants, processors, and retailers to the farm gate.
4. Access to contemporary technologies, extended services, and joint Goodwill training.
5. Agricultural Practices (GAP) and assuring agricultural produce traceability
6. Post-harvest losses can be reduced by combining storage and value addition facilities.
7. Adverse price fluctuations and distress sales can be handled or prevented if proper practises are followed.Contract farming arrangements, stocking in own common facilities or leased storage facilities with financial assistance, and so forth are examples.
8. Ease of communication for the spread of information about pricing and quantities in various areas, as well as other farming-related advises, decreasing formation asymmetries.
9. Access to institutional lending against shares without collateral due to the FPO framework's implicit shared liability.
10. As minimal scale economies are realised, movement up the value chain and graduation into primary and secondary processing will be possible.
11. Farmers will have more negotiating power, and production and processing operations will be more quality-oriented.

2.11 Broad Services and Activities to be undertaken by FPOs

The FPOs may provide and undertake following relevant major services and activities for their development as may be necessary-

(i) Supply quality production inputs like seed, fertilizer, pesticides and such other inputs at reasonably lower wholesale rates.

(ii) Make available need-based production and post-production machinery and equipment like cultivator, tiller, sprinkler set, combine harvester and such other machinery and equipment on custom hiring basis for members to reduce the per 2 unit production cost.

(iii) Make available value addition like cleaning, assaying, sorting, grading, packing and also farm level processing facilities at user charge basis on reasonably cheaper rate. Storage and transportation facilities may also be made available.

(iv) Undertake higher income generating activities like seed production, bee keeping, mushroom cultivation etc.

(v) Undertake aggregation of smaller lots of farmer-members' produce; add value to make them more marketable.

(vi) Facilitate market information about the produce for judicious decision in production and marketing.

(vii) Facilitate logistics services such as storage, transportation, loading/un-loading etc. on shared cost basis.

(viii) Market the aggregated produce with better negotiation strength to the buyers and in the marketing channels offering better and remunerative prices.

2.12 Principles of FPO

Fig. 2.3: Principles of FPO (Source: Govt. of Odisha)

2.13 FPO Promotion & Development Process

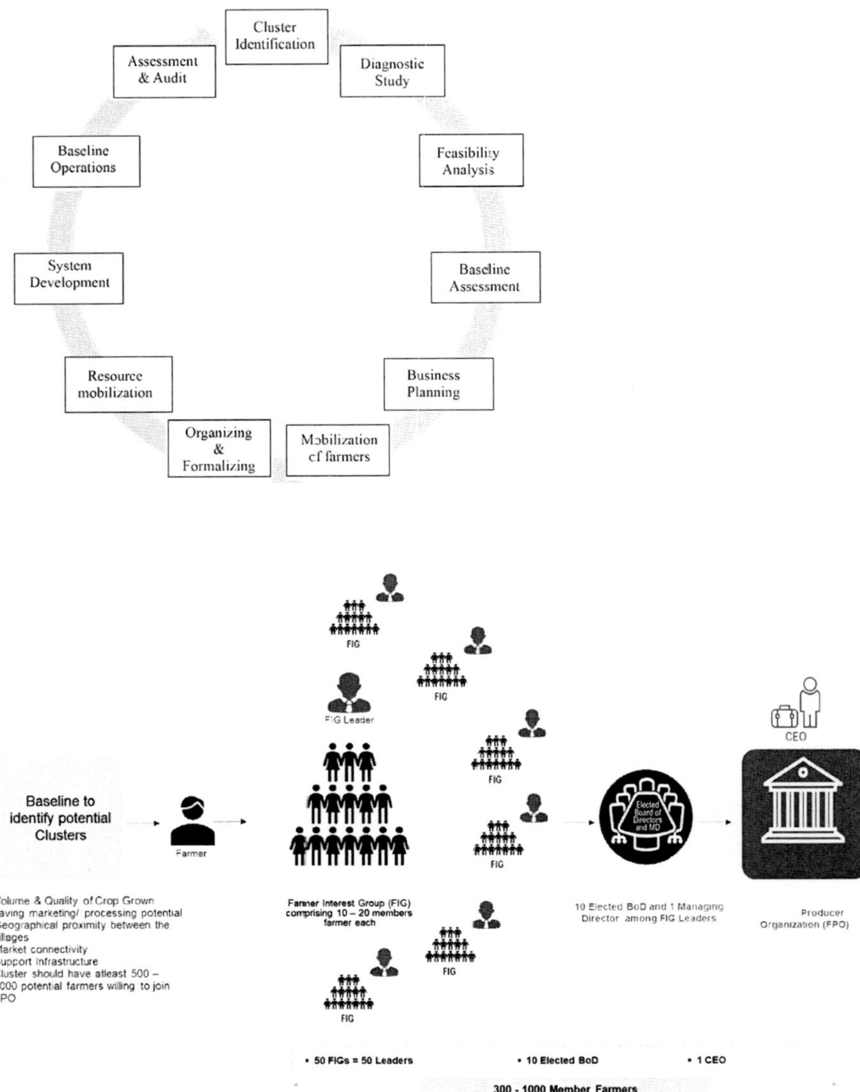

Fig. 2.4: Development & Process of FPO (Source: Govt. of Odisha)

2.14 FPO Ecosystem

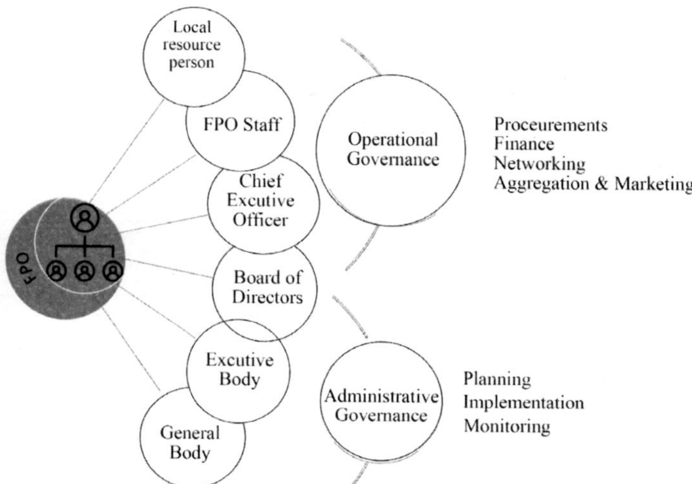

Fig. 2.5: FPO Ecosystem (*Source: Govt. of Odisha)*

2.15 Typology of FPOs

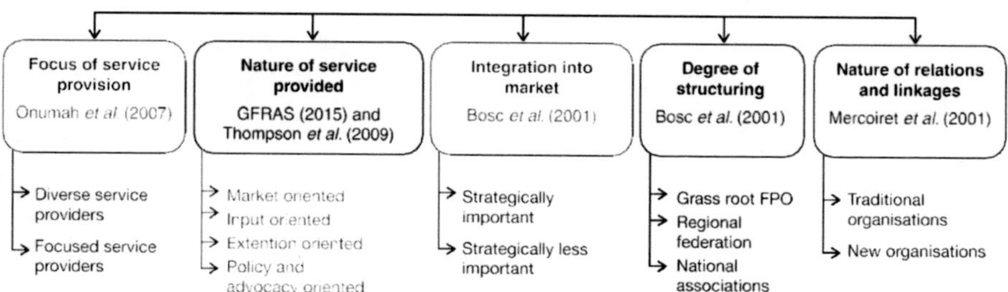

Fig. 2.6: Typology of FPO (Source: Govt. of Odisha)

2.16 Visualization of FPO in India

Presently, around 5000 FPOs (including FPCs) are in existence in the country. These were formed under various initiatives of the Govt. of India (including SFAC), State Governments, NABARD, as well as other organizations over the last 8-10 years. The vast majority of these FPOs are at their nascent stage and are still in the early growth phase of their life cycle. (MANAGE Report, 2019). It is estimated that at best 30%of these FPCs are currently operating viably and around 20% are still struggling to survive. Around 50% are still in the phase of mobilisation, equity collection, business planning other management related developmental stages This is quite comparable to the success rate vis-a-vis new enterprise start-ups in the industrial and processing sector in India. The number of FPO promoters is numerous and hence a representative listing of larger promoters is given here:

Table 2.15.1: Visualization of FPO in India

Sl. No	Promoting Agency	Nos.
1	SFAC	902
2	NABARD	2086
3	State Government (Funded by leveraging RKVY or the World Bank funds)	510
4	NRLM Programme (MoRD)	131
5	Other Organisations/Trust/Foundations	1371
Total		5000

Table 2.15.2: Visualization of FPO in Odisha

FPO Registered	**582**
Farmer Membership	223617
Districts covered	30
Blocks covered	206

2.17 Impact of FPO Promotion

In order to enhance farmers' income and empower small and marginal farmers, promotion of FPOs has evolved as an intervention strategy in India. The impact of related initiatives may be summarily considered as follows: -

a. FPOs are effectively lowering their procurement costs for insecticides, pesticides, fertilizers, and seeds by establishing inputs shops.

b. By offering specialized hiring services for agricultural equipment and machinery such as tractors, tillers, and harvesters, production and cultivation expenses are reduced.

c. FPOs increase the value of accruals to farmers by operating shared facilities for primary and secondary processing and direct selling.

d. Because they can supply volumes, they can directly bargain with and sell to major purchasers and retailers.

e. They can hedge against potential commodity price drops during harvest by launching a hedging strategy and utilizing the NCDEX platform.

f. By utilizing the e-NAM platform, FPOs may reach out to a large number of buyers in a cost-effective manner.

g. The market for organically produced commodities is being exploited through communal farming techniques, allowing supply of required volumes to access linked markets.

2.18 Challenges faced in the promotion of FPOs

Some of the more critical challenges confronting FPOs may be visualised as:

a. **Difficulty and delay in farmer mobilisation:** Some organisations active in promoting FPOs face significant attrition rates as well as capacity and competency shortages in organising FPOs. Furthermore, Boards of

Directors and FPO executives have a poor knowledge of business planning and the benefits of collective action.

b. **FPOs' low organisational and management capacity:** FPO boards of directors/leaders often have inadequate entrepreneurial and business management abilities. There is a need for capacity building and training of BoDs/leaders and FPO CEOs. This course includes not just effective company planning tools, but also enterprise management methods.

c. **Need for incubation and handholding support for FPOs:** FPOs struggle to network and negotiate with many stakeholders in order to accomplish their business plans, and as a result, they are unable to reap the benefits of economies of scale.

d. **An FPO's membership base:** In India, FPOs are sponsored by numerous organisations and have membership bases ranging from 50 to 1000 farmers. Developing an FPO with 1000 members takes time and might be tough at times.

e. **FPOs' restricted ability to generate adequate equity:** Currently, FPOs get a matching equity share (1:1) depending on the equity share mobilized from members up to Rs. 15 lakhs under the SFAC's Equity Grant Scheme. This is subject to a Rs. 1000 share restriction per farmer.

f. **Challenges at the policy level:** Today, there are various legislative barriers that prevent FPOs from reaping advantages owing to information asymmetry and a lack of knowledge. This is in terms of revising the state APMC statute, allowing FPOs to get direct market licenses, relaxing mandi cess, and relaxing filing statutory compliances, including those connected to the RoC and tax authorities. Penalty of delayed compliance is a burden, particularly on FPOs in their infancy.

g. **Limited ability to invest autonomously in primary/secondary processing, storage, and custom hiring facilities:** Due to limited access to equity or institutional funds at the outset, FPOs frequently face difficulties in establishing necessary infrastructure facilities to complement their business activities. They also confront difficulties in obtaining associated assistance from numerous government initiatives and ministries.

h. **FPOs' inability to get institutional finance without collateral:** Loan Guarantee cover of up to 85% of the applicable sanctioned credit facility (or) Rs. 85 Lakh, whichever is less, is guaranteed to Eligible Lending Institutions (ELIs) for each FPO borrower, subject to a maximum of twice during a 5-year period. However, considering the requirements of many FPOs, the maximum is rather modest. Also Banks have been reluctant to process cases of FPOs for Credit Guarantee by SFAC.

2.19 Institutional Innovation in Farmer Producer Organisation's Domain:

In India, PCs have tried several novel governance and management structures to deal with legal issues and manage their commercial success in a competitive setting. It is well understood that governance structure plays a significant role in ensuring that POs satisfy both member and corporate objectives (Harris et al., 1996). Some of them have raised more stock from members in order to develop member stakes and interest among other business entities in doing business with these firms. More equity may be mobilised from within the membership. For example, milk PCs offered by National Dairy Services (NDS, a subsidiary of the NDDB) have three membership tiers depending on patronage and equity investment (Singh, 2021).

Dividends can also be used to increase equity. Even in NDDB-promoted milk PCs, member equity dominates the capital structure, and strong earnings retention is practised to develop reserves and improve creditworthiness (Shah, 2016). Another distinguishing element of NDDB-promoted PCs in 2013 and 2014 was their magnitude, since they were at the state or sub-state level, spanning more than one district in general. Gujarat, Rajasthan, Andhra Pradesh, Punjab, and Uttar Pradesh are home to the five PCs. One of them is the all-women member PC in AP, which has over 40,000 members. They solely deal in milk and vary from other PCs in that they are supported by NDDB professionals and have their own governance structure.

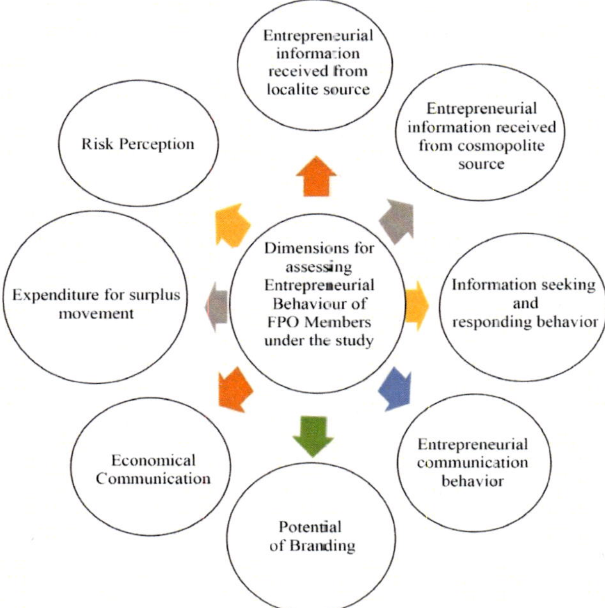

Fig. 2.6: Conceptual Framework of the study

It is worth noting that the Farmer's Produce Trade and Commerce Act of 2020, as well as the Agricultural and Livestock Produce Marketplaces (APLM) promotion and facilitation Acts at the state level, allow for private markets and e-markets by FPOs—mostly PCs. This was formerly permitted under the Agriculture Produce Market Committee (APMC) Acts, where such companies may establish private wholesale marketplaces, and a few hundred of such markets have been established by PCs in Maharashtra. This is also an innovative practise in engaging with the market and bringing the market closer to farmers, as well as protecting their market interests by providing an alternative channel, in addition to bringing market orientation and confidence among member farmers that they can use such markets to create more jobs at local level.Similarly, some PCs in West Bengal operating Sufal Bangla stores as franchisees is a novel approach to achieve scale and farmer advantage (Singh, 2021). Franchising is a cost-cutting strategy for agricultural inputs and services, as well as output handling. Many PCs and agricultural start-ups have utilised this for some time now, and more PCs should embrace it (Singh, 2016)

3

Citations on FPO and Entrepreneurial Communication

In any scientific investigation and research, a comprehensive review of literature is very essential. Its main function, apart from determining the work done before concerning the problem area i.e., area of investigation, to provide an insight into the methods and procedures and create a basis for interpretation of findings. As direct references of all the items are not in abundance, certain specific references along with some indirect references have been incorporated in this chapter for the purpose of meaningful use. In the present study, reviews of literature have been summarized in the following table

Sl. No.	Author	Year	Important Revelations
1	Acharya *et.al.*	2022	The correlation coefficients suggest that younger respondents have recorded higher and better entrepreneurial behaviour and this have also been reflected in Experience in SHG. Regression results found that 11 casual variables together have contributed 65.8 per cent of variance in consequent variable Entrepreneurial behaviour (y_1). Extension contacts (x_7) Distance from market (x_{10}), No of trainings attended (x8) has been retained in the last step of step down regression that means these are the most important causal variables which affect the consequent variable. The results of path analysis envies that the variable No of trainings attended (x_8) have got highest indirect effect on y_1.
2	Gurjar *et.al.*	2022	The study revealed that the majority 59.00 per cent of the beekeeping farmers had medium information seeking behaviour towards beekeeping farming. About 22.50 per cent of beekeeping farmers had low information seeking behaviour towards beekeeping farming and 18.50 per cent respondents had high information seeking behaviour towards beekeeping farming.
3	Sun *et.al.*	2022	The results indicate that awareness has a significant positive effect on consumers' purchase intention and that brand trust could strengthen the influence of awareness on consumers' purchase intention. At the same time, brand trust can promote the positive influence of perceived quality on consumers' purchase intention.

Sl. No.	Author	Year	Important Revelations
			This study extends the research on consumer behaviour theory, reveals the influence mechanism of consumer purchase intention of the agricultural products of regional public brands, and provides a new perspective for further research on agricultural products in some regions
4	Nwachukwu	2022	The findings of study revealed that agripreneurship marketing has a significant positive impact on economic recovery in terms of increasing GDP and creating employment.
5	Khose *et.al.*	2022	The result of the study showed that, 43.33 per cent of respondents belonged to middle age group, 28.33 per cent of respondents educated up to junior college level, majority of 60.00 per cent of the respondents had Agriculture as a occupation, 61.67 per cent of respondents had annual income up to Rs.3,33,333, 38.33 per cent of respondents possessed semi-medium land holding, 50.00 per cent of respondents had put up to 0.36 ha area under ginger crop, 91.67 per cent of respondents had well or tube well as their source of irrigation, 70.00 per cent, 55.00 per cent and 58.33 per cent respondents had medium extension contact, medium social participation and scientific orientation, respectively. Majority of 73.33 per cent of respondents had medium level of entrepreneurial behaviour. Whereas majority of 90.00 per cent of respondents faced constraints of fluctuating prices of ginger in market.
6	Singh *et.al.*	2022	The findings revealed that the members (including management) of the functional FPOs had higher risk bearing capacity, greater economic motivation and more innovativeness as compared to the respondents from non-functional FPOs. Similarly, respondents from functional FPOs were socially, economically and managerially more empowered than the non-functional FPOs. Business skills of the members, including the managerial members, of functional FPOs were also better as compared to those from the non-functional FPOs. Regression estimates revealed that the functionality, better academic qualification, bigger land holding and joint family system were responsible for the higher net annual income of the respondents.
7	Singh *et.al.*	2022	The study revealed that organisational structure has an explanatory effect on relationship between the shareholders and performance of the FPOs as the former infuuences the information flow and decision making in the organisation. The structural framework was explained with help of a flow chart. Organisational characteristics of the FPOs were identified and it was revealed that the participation in the meetings, awareness about the meeting agenda and involvement in decision making of the members were statistically diferent in functional vis-à-vis non-functional FPOs The study revealed

Sl. No.	Author	Year	Important Revelations
			that organisational structure has an explanatory effect on relationship between the shareholders and performance of the FPOs as the former influences the information flow and decision making in the organisation. The structural framework was explained with help of a flow chart. Organisational characteristics of the FPOs were identified and it was revealed that the participation in the meetings, awareness about the meeting agenda and involvement in decision making of the members were statistically different in functional vis-à-vis non-functional FPOs.
8	Dechamma *et.al.*	2022	It was found that as high as 36.67 per cent of farmers possessed more favourable attitude towards FPOs, while 35.83 and 27.50 per cent of farmers possessed less favourable and favourable attitude towards FPOs, respectively. The VHFPC members had attitude mean score of 69.67 and the AHFPC members had the attitude mean score as 80.67, thus there is a significant difference at one per cent level with the t- value of 12.34 between VHFPC members and AHFPC members' attitude towards the farmers producer organization.
9	Harikrishna *et.al.*	2022	More and more contribution from the promoting institutions is of utmost need for education, business planning and market linkage with various national and international companies. FPOs have better opportunities for direct marketing which is a need of the hour for the people of villages. Direct marketing support farmers to lessen transportation costs and permits them to progress price realization. Support from the policymakers in running the FPO will be a great boon to the farming community.
10	Shreedutt and Mazhar	2022	The findings of the study revealed that 62.50 per cent of the respondents belonged to the middle- aged group, 41.66 per cent of the respondents belong to the farming occupation and majority of the respondents (55 %) belongs to medium level of annual income i.e. 50,000 – 1 lakh. The findings also revealed that 63.34 per cent of the respondents had medium level of entrepreneurial behaviour followed by 15.83 % and 20.83 % of the respondents with low and high levels of entrepreneurial behaviour respectively.
11	Dey *et.al.*	2022	The survey findings highlights that marketable surplus directly escalates with increase in farm size. Factors such as family consumption, wages in kind and animal feed reduced the amount of surplus available for marketing. The disposal pattern clearly indicates that due to shortage of proper storage facilities, transportation and credit facilities a large number of farmers vend their produce to village traders immediately after the harvest. Proper technological developments are key to increase the marketable surplus in the area.

Sl. No.	Author	Year	Important Revelations
12	Uzelac *et.al.*	2022	Creation of a more desirable image of an agricultural product most often has a strong reflection on the area of origin, as well as on reformation of the social attitude towards that environment. Branded products and services have a higher market value, due to which legal aspects enabling not only branding, but maintenance of a brand as well, are of special significance.
13	Roy and Acharya	2021	The social ecology of entrepreneurial communication is comprising of farm production process, technology back up, input and credit delivery mechanism, operating supply chain, market segmentation, decision support system and policy formulation for both micro and macro-sociological realities.
14	Amitha *et.al.*	2021	The results of the study revealed that under group composition, majority were small farmers with middle age (55.55%), primary school education (35.55%), with medium farming experience (47.77%) and with medium annual income (60.00%). Majority of respondents perceived that with respect to management and governance characteristics of FPO had poor group leadership (41.11%), fair group communication (58.88%) and medium adherence to rules(41.11%). With respect to membership commitment majority of respondents had low group participation (43.33%), medium group cohesiveness (47.77%) and low team spirit (43.33%).
15	Prasad *et.al.*	2021	It was revealed from present investigation that majority of dairy farmers had highest entrepreneurial behaviour towards the innovativeness and decision making ability. Majority of the dairy farmers belonged to medium level of entrepreneurial behaviour, followed by low level of entrepreneurial behaviour of dairy farmers. Therefore, there is a need for providing adequate awareness and training programme for dairy farmers to help them develop into successful entrepreneur.
16	Rath *et.al.*	2021	FPOs can address the problems related to the farm by collective action in terms of procuring the vegetable crops like brinjal, bitter gourd, okra, snake gourd, drumstick, tomatoes and others from the farmers, took the same in vans to sell to individual households. If vegetables are limited in supply or not available, FPO can bring them from the nearby local markets and supply to the customers. By approaching the consumers directly, farmers can market their produce easily because of which the farmers share in consumers rupee can be increased and thus there can be Agriculture and Food ESN Publications ISBN: 978-93-90781-05-8 Page 19 improvement in the standard of living of the farmers amidst this global crisis.

Sl. No.	Author	Year	Important Revelations
17	Reddy, A.A.	2021	For farmers organizations to be successful, they have to have least cost models, high turn-over, continuous cash flow to meet working expenses, value added products, bulk institutional sales and enhancing branded retail sales
18	Raveesha *et.al.*	2021	The net return per rupee of water, the net return per kg of output, is higher in both GWTI and GWCI compared to GWSI. Considering the income from Agriculture, non-agriculture and livestock, the net return per acre of net cropped area is the highest in GWTI and GWCI compared with GWSI. This shows that in addition to agriculture, the GWTI and GWCI farms have exhibited efficiency even in non agriculture and livestock sources of income when compared with medium and large farmers. The incremental net return is computed between GWTI and GWSI, it turns to be positive for all sample farmers. The supply of water through channel system has contributed substantially for farmers who are totally dependent on agriculture.
19	Singh *et.al.*	2021	the unfavourable attitude of most of the respondents of non-functional FPOs is probably due to lack of trust, cooperation and conflict management among the members thus the efforts are required to convert the covert attitude into overt behaviour so as to harness the potentials of the FPOs in the State.
20	Babu & Patoju	2021	It was also found that services provided by FPCs like marketing, value addition, technological services and preharvest services were satisfactory, while agricultural advisory services, capacity building and credit access services were poor. A model ACITM (Agriculture Advisory, Capacity Building, Technological and Marketing Services) is suggested to be executed by the FPCDN (Farmer Producer Companies Development Network) – a development network consortium for addressing FPCs problems and strengthening the FPCs.
21	Selvaraj, N.	2021	During this study area farmers, were found to not attach importance to fertilizers and pesticides. The farmers are cognizant of their importance but thanks to insufficient funds, they're unable to use fertilizers and pesticides as per the recommendations of the agricultural scientists. Besides, per annum the prices of fertilizers and pesticides keep increasing. Hence, it's suggested that costs of fertilizer and pesticides should be reduced, or they'll be applied to farmers at subsidized rates.
22	Dhineshwari *et.al.*	2021	According to the results, it is concluded that the majority of the sample Farmer Producer Companies are in distress zone and if the present circumstance proceeded, these organizations will be bankrupt, within next two years and all of the companies have negative sustainable growth rate, indicating that they

Sl. No.	Author	Year	Important Revelations
			would be unable to operate without external funding. As a result, there is an urgent need to concentrate on these companies in order to ensure their sustainable growth.
23	Nerisa Paladan	2021	Findings reveal that farmers and fisherfolks have a moderate entrepreneurial competency; both rank first the risk-taking and goal setting as the least. Farmer self-confidence increases as they age while for fisherfolks it declines; male farmers are more persuasive, farmers with business experience have higher competency for opportunity seeking and risk-taking, and farmers' competency differs in terms of their educational attainment. While fisherfolks show no difference in entrepreneurial competency for both men and women, with or without business experience, and only the competency for persistence differ in their educational attainment. Developing a framework for implementing community-based enterprise should focus on intensifying the entrepreneurial competency of farmers and fisherfolks.
24	Li *et.al.*	2021	The results show that: (1) There is a significant and positive correlation between entrepreneurial motivation and entrepreneurial performance. (2) Entrepreneurial motivation, work experience and entrepreneurial training have a significant positive impact on entrepreneurial performance. (3) Entrepreneurial ability has a positive moderating effect on the impact of entrepreneurial motivation on entrepreneurial performance.
25	Zhang *et.al.*	2021	The government judges distribution according to the awareness of agricultural onlinebrand products' establishment by the farmer and the e-retailer, and subsidizes them with ex post strategy.
26	K.M.V. Sachithra	2020	This study revealed a moderate level of entrepreneurial behaviour of the farmers. They have shown their attraction towards risk taking; however, practical issues were there that restricted farmers from change-orientation to utilizing opportunities. Further, there was a statistically significant influence of entrepreneurial behaviour to financial performance of cinnamon crop farms. According to the interviews, the farm owners who showed entrepreneurial behaviour are equipped with the skills of learning by doing, centralised decision-making, targeting and analyzing market trends.
27	Madhumita *et.al.*	2020	This study revealed that nearly half (47%) of the women agripreneurs fall under medium level of entrepreneurial behaviour, 7 per cent under high and 6 per cent under low level of entrepreneurial behaviour. It also depicted that educational status, dependency ratio, enterprises related trainings attended by women agripreneurs, mass media exposure,

Sl. No.	Author	Year	Important Revelations
			cosmopoliteness, extension participation and credit orientation of women agripreneurs had positive and significant relationship with their entrepreneurial behaviour.
28	Jamir & Jha	2020	Findings revealed that majority (71.67 %) of the respondent had medium level of entrepreneurial behaviour. Correlation analysis revealed that variables viz., income from king chilli cultivation and attitude of farmers had positive and highly significant association with the entrepreneurial behaviour of the respondents. It was also found that variables viz., family size, size of landholding under agriculture, annual income and adoption had positive and significant association with the entrepreneurial behaviour of the respondents. The variable income from king chilli cultivation and attitude were found important in terms of determining the entrepreneurial behavioural pattern of king chilli farmers.
29	Pongener & Jha	2020	The study revealed that majority (72%) of the respondents had medium level of achievement motivation, innovativeness (71%) and planning orientation (62%). Majority (91%) of them had medium level of risk orientation, management orientation (84%), marketing orientation (81%) and decision making ability (78%). It was also found that majority (67%) of them had medium level of entrepreneurial behaviour. Variables age, education, size of land holding under agriculture and experience in off-season cucumber cultivation had significant association with the entrepreneurial behaviour of the respondents. The study concluded that organizing awareness and motivation programmes on entrepreneurship development shall be helpful in increasing the productivity and profitability of the cucumber farmers.
30	Roy *et.al.*	2020	The study revealed that to move toward comparatively high-end technology, such as drip irrigation and improved packaging and storage. Farmers who are members of FPOs, in which farmers' and managers' incentives are comparatively aligned, are more successful in adopting new technology and better managing their risks.
31	Mubarak *et.al.*	2019	The results showed that entrepreneurial competence negatively affects entrepreneurial intentions with a coefficient value of -0.472 with a significance value on 0,29 which means significant at 0.005. Likewise, the variables of entrepreneurial characteristics have a positive effect on entrepreneurial intentions with a coefficient value of 0.789 with a significance value on 0.12 which means significant at 0.005.

Sl. No.	Author	Year	Important Revelations
32	Manaswi *et.al.*	2019	The findings indicate that the input use in production of chilli was much less for the members of FPOs due to adoption of low inputs organic farming practices. Despite a lower yield, the members could realize 13.86% higher gross returns primarily attributed to FPOs providing access to technology and markets. The farmers in the study regions were following three marketing channels for disposal of their produce. The channel that involved FPOs with member farmers on the one end and consumers on the other is found to have the highest marketing efficiency in organic chilli.
33	Sharma *et.al.*	2019	The Study concludes that FPOs play a positive role and leads to enhanced income for farmers by providing them with access to institutional credit, informed and better decisions, access to better and improved inputs, effectiveness &efficiency in farming operations and better marketing facilities; there still remains challenges and policy gaps that are unaddressed. Few of the major challenges faced by institutions and government agencies in building strong and sustainable FPOs include inadequacies related to professional management, access to credit, risk mitigation mechanism, accessibility to market, alongside weak financials and lack of technical skill and awareness among users of FPOs.
34	Manaswi *et.al.*	2018	The findings indicated that more than 50% of total mobilised farmers belonging to four states namely Karnataka, Madhya Pradesh, Tamil Nadu and West Bengal. The highest number of promoting institutions have found in Karnataka (85) constituting about 8.9 % of the total promoting agencies functioning in the country. The number of FPOs promoting institutions per gross cropped area, ease of doing business, number of markets, KCC per operational holding and rural literacy are significant factors having bearing on the performance of the states
35	Plastina *et.al.*	2018	The average net returns to cover crop use for farmers who did not use cover crops for grazing livestock or forage were consistently negative across different planting and termination methods, tillage practices, and experience levels. Only farmers who used cover crops for grazing livestock or forage and received cost-share payments tended to derive net positive returns from cover crop use.
36	Suryawanshi, O.P.	2018	Value addition of rice to different product enhances the original market price of the rice but it needs investment. A small or marginal farmer cannot invest the huge amount of equipment cost for processing. So, for the investment on paddy processing equipment/ machineries an entrepreneur may introduces in paddy processing field. These investments

Sl. No.	Author	Year	Important Revelations
			may enhance the income of an entrepreneur or group of farmers. Agreement between an entrepreneur and farmer can fulfil the needs of farmer as well as entrepreneur. In this study various methods of value addition of rice are described as well.
37	Marina *et.al.*	2018	Majority of the respondents (87%) finds origin of the product very important while at the same time 79,5% of them are not aware of quality labels and trademarks of agricultural and food products in Croatia. 77,5% of the respondents consider products bearing quality labels more reliable than those without, especially on the EU level. Only 2.6 % of the respondents agree with the statement that Croatian products bearing quality labels are promoted sufficiently, 61,5% do not agree and 35,9% agree that there is a need to improve promotional activities. The response indicates that the promotion of such products is not sufficient in spite of the fact that consumers are willing to pay even higher prices for quality (74,9% responses). The awareness of consumers about specific agricultural products labelled with designated origin of Croatia varies from 22,6% (Meat of Croatian Farms), 45,2% (Eggs of Croatian Farms) to 71% (Zagreb fresh cow cheese) 4 Associated with the verse of Croatian hymn and 77,4% (Zagreb Cherry).
38	Shirur et.al	2017	Five attributes of farmers and their units, six attributes of socio-psychological traits and four extension variables were studied for investigating their effect on entrepreneurial behaviour of the respondents. Regression analysis showed that, academic qualification, cosmopolitanism, self-reliance, mass media participation, extension participation and training were significantly contributing to the entrepreneurial behaviour of the respondents.
39	Ahuja *et.al.*	2016	The results revealed that only age of the farmers was negatively and significantly correlated with entrepreneurial behaviour while all other variables i.e., educational qualification, size of land holding, annual income, caste, dairy farming experience, extension contact, social participation, mass media exposure, economic motivation, scientific orientation, attitude towards dairy farming and market orientation were found to have positive and significant relationship with entrepreneurial behaviour. The regression analysis further revealed that educational qualification, mass media exposure and economic motivation were the important predictors of entrepreneurial behaviour of dairy farmers. All the thirteen independent variables fitted in the regression analysis explained 95.42% of variation towards entrepreneurial behaviour of dairy farmers.

Sl. No.	Author	Year	Important Revelations
40	Datta *et.al.*	2016	Result shows that 58.75 percent women have medium level of entrepreneurial behaviour followed by 25 percent have low and 16.25 percent have high level of entrepreneurial behaviour. Study also indicated that expenditure, annual income, credit orientation, extension participation, mass media participation has positive significant relationship with entrepreneurial behaviour at 1 % level of significance whereas level of aspiration have positive significant relationship at 5% level of significance. So, women should be encouraged through providing financial support, various training programme, marketing support etc. to make their more involvement in entrepreneurship development and improve their socio-economic condition.
41	Abeyrathne & Jayawardena	2014	Study revealed effective entrepreneurial behaviour involving high planning ability, and decision making ability Majority of the farmers were at a moderate level of innovativeness, risk orientation, coordinating ability, opportunity seeking behaviour, self-confidence, achievement motivation, and cosmopolitanism. Group interactions were moderate at seasonal planning, and in selecting of crops. Group interactions were low in land preparation, pest and disease controlling, harvesting, irrigation water distribution, participating in training programmes, and selling. Entrepreneurial behaviour of farmers has enhanced with group interactions. The two farmer groups had significant differences in group interactions and entrepreneurial behaviour due to group characteristics. It is recommended to improve group interactions through awareness programmes, and small group formation activities.
42	Kacharu	2013	Based on his study on entrepreneurial behaviour of floriculturist revealed that 63.34 per cent of respondents had medium entrepreneurial behaviour, 20 per cent and 15.83 per cent of respondents had high and low entrepreneurial behaviour respectively.
43	Minten *et.al.*	2013	Two types of brands can be distinguished, i.e. low-price and high-price brands. Low-costs brands focus exclusively on attractive glossy packing with little consideration for quality. Investments, but profits as well, are small. The high-price brands pay attention to quality beyond packing, invest in advertisements and promotion, explore options for value-addition, and employ specialized salesmen. We find that there are little direct benefits to the farmers from the emergence of these brands. However, farmers might benefit indirectly because of the expanding product demand.

Sl. No.	Author	Year	Important Revelations
44	Jha, K.K.	2012	Major findings revealed that in terms of entrepreneurial attributes, majority of the pineapple growers possessed high level of self confidence, low level of scientific orientation and medium level of knowledge about improved practices of pineapple cultivation, economic motivation, farm decision making ability and risk orientation. The variables namely – indigenous knowledge, farm decision-making ability, self-confidence and economic motivation were found important in influencing the entrepreneurial attributes of the pineapple growers
45	Jha, K.K.	2012	The study revealed that majority of the potato cultivators had medium level of knowledge about improved package of practices of potato cultivation, farm decision making ability, family size, economic motivation, marketing orientation and scientific orientation. The entrepreneurial behaviour of the potato growers were significantly influenced by their knowledge, farm decision making ability, family size and economic motivation. The study contributes to the knowledge about designing relevant training programmes giving due cognizance to the influencing variables.
46	Naveen	2012	From his study on entrepreneurial behaviour of pomegranate farmers revealed that 39.17 per cent of respondents had medium entrepreneurial behaviour, 35 per cent and 25.83 per cent of the respondents had high and low entrepreneurial behaviour respectively.
47	Nwaiwu	2012	Results showed that the mean age, level of education, household size, farming experience and farm size were 51years, 12years, 6 persons, 23years, and 0.511 hectares respectively. The results also showed that labour cost took the highest proportion with 61.17% of the total expenses incurred in garden egg production, while marketing charges took the lowest proportion with 1.25%. The mean net return per hectare from garden egg production was N105, 140.07. The results also showed that cost of agro-chemicals and size of farm land were the major determinants of net returns from garden egg production by showing a statistically significant effect at 5% level. Provision of these inputs in adequate quantities and at affordable prices will ensure enhanced net returns from garden egg production.
48	Ommani, A.R.	2011	Based on the results of SWOT, strategies for farming system management were prioritized and they include: development of poor local market opportunities and infrastructure, planting of crops with high economic values, development of governmental supports, preparing strategic plans for development of organic farming, considering the quality of

Sl. No.	Author	Year	Important Revelations
			crops, considering farm sustainability indexes, using sustainable water resources management and development of extension programs based on farmers' needs.
49	Beebe and Darling	2007	revealed that The keys to achieving acceptable levels of excellence involve four key entrepreneurial leadership strategies : attention through vision, meaning through communication, trust through positioning and confidence through trust.
50	Palanivelu and Rajanarayanan	2005	defined entrepreneur as a person who makes an attempt to enhance the value of the product by introducing innovations and combining the factors of production.

4

Social Ecology and FPO

4.1 Research Setting

In any social science research, it is hardly possible to conceptualize and perceive the data and interpret the data more accurately until and unless a clear understanding of the characteristics in the area and attitude or the behavior of people is at commend of the interpreter who intends to unveil an understanding of the implication and behavioral complexes of the individual who live in the area under reference and form a representative part of the larger community. The socio-demographic background of the local people in a rural setting has been critically administered in this section. A research setting is a surrounding in which input and elements of research are contextually imbibed, interactive and mutually contributive to the system performance. Research setting is immensely important in the sense because it is characterizing and influencing the interplays of different factors and components.

The present study was taken up in the Nayagarh district of Odisha. The study was carried out in Ranpur block from Nayagarh district. In Ranpur block, 2 Farmer Producer Organisations were selected for the study. A brief description of the whole study area has been provided in this chapter.

4.2 Area of study

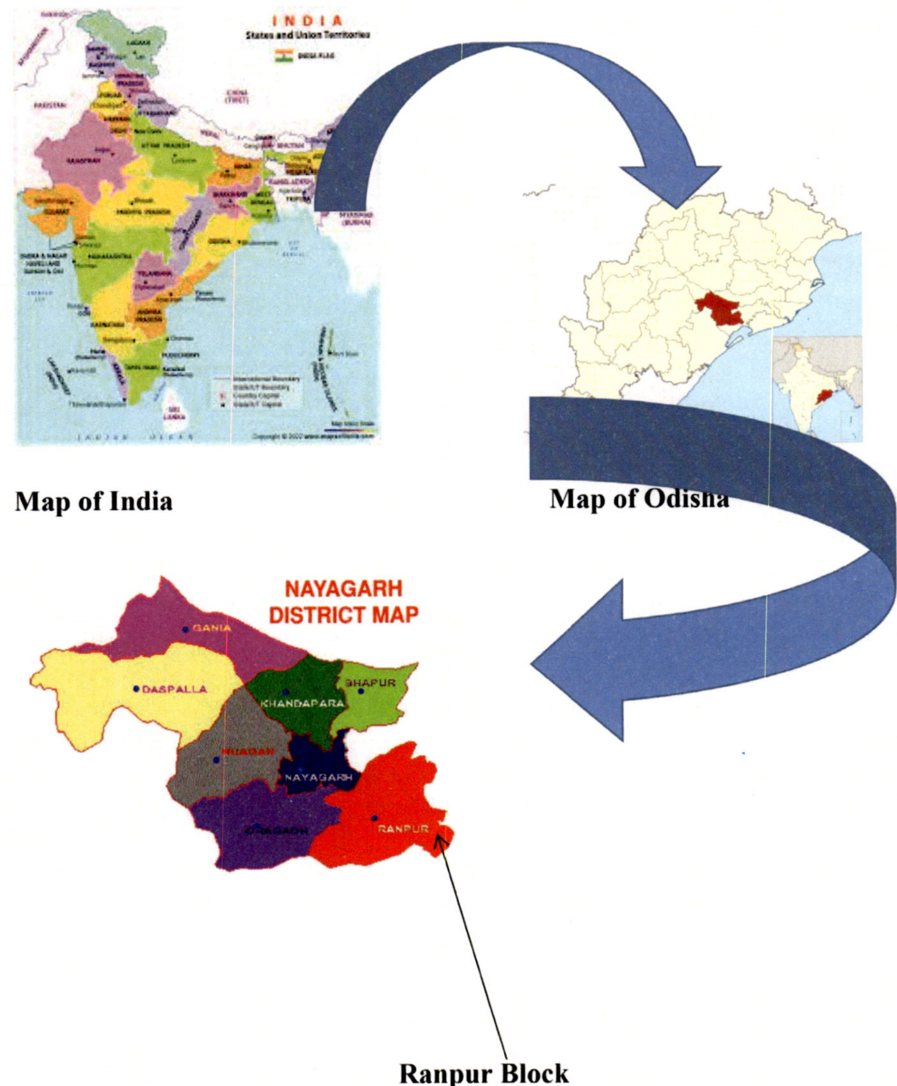

Map 4.2.1: Area of study :Ranpur Block, Nayagarh district, Odisha, India

4.3 Profile of the state, Odisha

The state of Odisha was formed on 1st April, 1936. Odisha is divided into 30 districts for administrative convenience. These are again regrouped into 3 revenue divisions (Central, Southern and Northern).

- **Central Division** comprises of Cuttack, Jagatsinghpur, Kendrapada, Jajpur, Balasore, Bhadrak, Puri, Khordha, Nayagarh, and Mayurbhanj

- **Southern Division** includes Ganjam, Gajapati, Koraput, Nabarangpur, Rayagada, Malkangiri, Kalahandi, Nuapada, Kandhamal, and Boudh districts
- **Northern Division** covers Sambalpur, Deogarh, Jharsuguda, Bargarh, Bolangir, Sonepur, Sundargrh, Dhenkanal, Angul, and Keonjhar

Odisha has 58 sub-divisions, 317 tahasils and 314 blocks. These 314 blocks comprise of 6,801 Gram Panchayats & 51,349 villages. There are 5 Municipal Corporations, 45 Municipalities, 60 Notified Area Councils and 2 Industrial towns. There are 583 numbers of Police Stations and 317 No. of Fire Stations. The State is divided into 21 no. of Lok Sabha Constituencies and 147 no. of Assembly Constituencies.

The areas of the state north of latitude 20°N have elevation up to 500m above sea level, in general and in the south western districts, they rise to 1500-1600m above sea level. The eastern hill are elevated and are generally 900 m above sea level. It is surrounded by West Bengal in the north-east, Bihar and Jharkhand in the north, Andhra Pradesh in the south-east, Chhattisgarh in the west and Bay of Bengal in the east.

4.3.1 Demographic Features

As per 2011 census, Odisha has 96, 61,085 number of households which is 3.9 percentage of the total number of households of India. The total population of the state is 4,19,74,218 (male-2,12,12,136 female-2,07,62,082), out of which 3,49,70,562 (83 %) lives in rural areas. The share of ST and SC population to total state population is 22.8 percent and 17.1 percent respectively. The decadal growth rate (2001-2011) of population is 14.0 and the density of population per sq km is 270. Odisha has a sex ratio (females per 1000 males) of 979. The child sex ratio (0-6 years) is 941. Odisha attained the literacy rate of 72.87 percent at par with the national average 72.99 percent in 2011 census registering a decadal increase of 9.8 percent between 2001 and 2011. The State's male literacy rate of 81.59 percent was marginally higher and female literacy rate of 64 percent was also at par with national averages by 2011. The SC and ST communities had relatively lower literacy rate of 69.02 and 52.24 percent in 2011.

4.3.2 Climate of Odisha

The State has a tropical climate, characterised by high temperature, high humidity, medium to high rainfall and short mild winters. The year may be divided into four seasons. The winter season from December to February is followed by the pre-monsoon or hot weather season from March to May. The period from June to September constitutes the southwest monsoon season and the period of October and November is the post-monsoon season. During the period from December to February, generally low temperatures prevail over the state except in the coastal belt. In the hot weather season from March to May, weather is generally dry and uncomfortable in the interior, while due to lower temperatures, the plateau regions are comparatively less uncomfortable. The normal rainfall of the State is 1,451.2 mm. The actual rainfall received, vary from district to district. About 75 percent to 80 percent of rainfall is received during the period from June to September. Even though the quantum of rain fall is quite high, its distribution during the monsoon period is highly uneven and erratic. As a result, flood and drought visit regularly with varying intensity. By mid-October, the south-west monsoon generally withdraws from Odisha.

The State can be divided into ten agro-climatic zones on the basis of soil, weather and other relevant characteristics. Its land can be classified into three categories, low (25.6%), medium (33.6%) and up-lands (40.8%) with various types of soils like red, yellow, red-loamy, alluvial, coastal alluvial, laterite and black soil, etc. with low and medium texture.

4.3.3 Agriculture Scenario of the State

Odisha is an Agrarian State. Almost 70 per cent population of the State are dependent on agriculture. The agriculture sector contributes only about 26 per cent of the Gross State Domestic Product (GSDP), with more than 70% population dependence resulting in low per capita income in the farm sector. he State has about 64.09 lakh hectares of cultivable area out of total geographical area of 155.711 lakh hectares, accounting for 41.16 percent. Total cultivated area is about 61.50 lakh hectares. About 40.17 lakh hectares of cultivable area has acidic soil and approx. 4.00 lakh hectares suffers from salinity. About 3.00 lakh hectares of cultivable area suffers from water logging. Agriculture contributes about 26% in the State Gross Domestic Product (SGDP). About 65% of the workforce depends on agriculture for their employment.

The average size of holding in the State is 1.25 ha. The small and marginal farmers constitute about 83% of the farming community.

The average rainfall in the State is 1452 mm, of which about 80% is confined to monsoon months (June-September). The total irrigation potential created is 27.63 lakh hectares in Kharif and 13.31 lakh hectares in Rabi.

The total food grain production in the State during 2007-08 is estimated to be 92.13 lakh tones which is approx. 4.06 percent of national food grain production. Agriculture in Odisha is characterized by low productivity on account of various factors. These factors include problematic soil (acidic, saline & waterlogged), lack of assured irrigation, low seed replacement rate, low level of fertilizer consumption (53 kg/ha. against national average of 113 kg/ha.), low level of mechanization etc. The serious gaps in yield potential and the technology transfer provide an opportunity to the State to increase production and productivity substantially.

4.3.4. Soil of the State

Odisha is a state with different physiographic and agro-climatic zones. Soils are generally fertile, but some are deficient. Soils of Odisha are mainly developed by the relief, parent material and climate. The biotic features, mainly the natural vegetation follows the climatic pattern. Soils of Odisha have been classified in to 8 broad soil groups. They are Red soils, Laterite and Lateritic soils, Red and Yellow soils, Coastal salt affected alluvial soils, Deltaic alluvial soils, Black soil, Brown forest soils. The soils of Odisha have problematic one and classified in to 3 classes i.e.

(a) Upland, low fertile, low water retentive acidic soils.

(b) Lowland soils posing iron toxicity problems

(c) Coastal salt affected soils

4.3.5 Agro-climatic Zones of Odisha

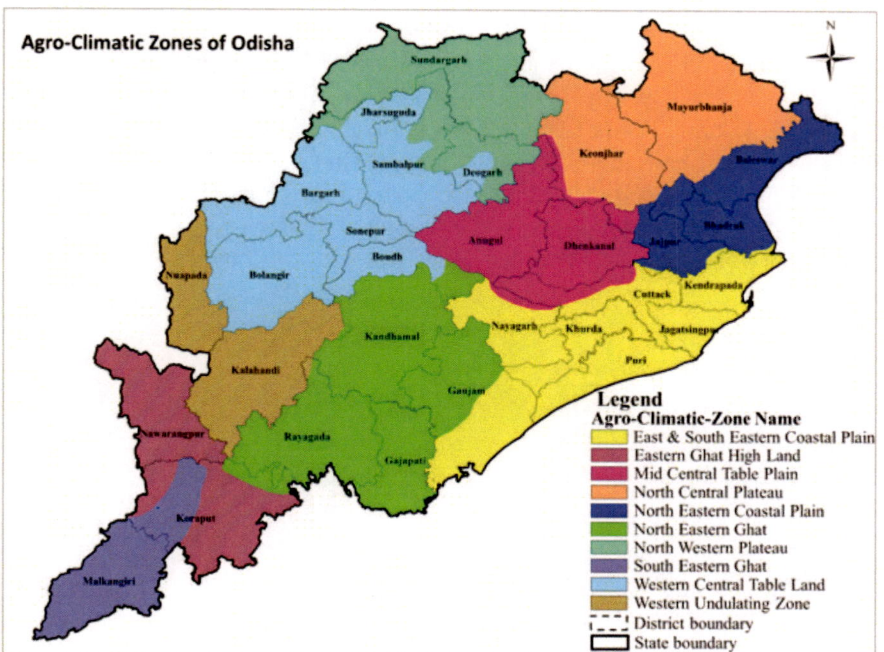

Map 4.3.5.1: Agroclimatic zones of Odisha

(Source : Govt of Odisha)

Integrating the effect of land from topography, climate, soils and crop adaptability, the state is divided in to 10 agroclimatic zones.

Table 4.1: Agro□climatic zones & soil group

SI.NO.	Zone	Broad Soil Group
1	North-western plateau	Mixed red and yellow
2	North-central plateau	Red
3	North-Eastern coastal plain	Coastal alluvial
4	East and South-Eastern coastal plain	Deltaic alluvial and laterite
5	North-Eastern Ghat	Red loam and brown forest
6	Eastern Ghat high land	Red and laterite
7	South-Eastern Ghat	Red
8	Western undulating	Red and black
9	West-Central table land	Mixed red and black
10	Mid-Central table land	Red and laterite

4.3.6 Major Crops Grown in the State

The state Odisha produces a number of crops. Kharif is the main cropping season in Odisha and rice is the principal crop which occupies 67percent of the cultivated land. But cropping during Rabi season is confined to the irrigated tracts and lands with available residual moisture in the soil, which mostly depends on the occurrence of rainfall during the last part of September. The other major crops grown are Maize, Ragi, Pulses, (Arhar, Mung, Biri), Oilseeds (Groundnut, Til, Mustard, Niger) , Fibres(Jute, Mesta, Cotton), Sugarcane, Vegetables, spices and Fruit crops(Mango, Coconut, Cashew nut).In area and production , Odisha is first in ranking in Brinjal production. Again in Odisha Sugarcane cultivation has been widely accepted by the farmers.

Table 4.2: Major crops grown in the state Odisha

Crops	Area (lakh ha)	Production (lakh ha)	Productivity(kg/ha)
Rice	43.65	70.22	1609
Maize	2.28	4.99	2191
Total cereals	48.28	77.45	1604
Pulses	20.92	9.62	460
Oilseeds	7.97	6.19	776
Sugarcane	0.37	26.12	70852
Ground nut	2.43	3.99	1639
Total vegetables	6.94	89.62	12910
Turmeric	0.25	1.89	7478
Chillies	0.75	0.64	852
Sweet potato	0.50	4.39	8696
Cotton	0.54	1.47	464

4.4 Description of Nayagarh District

Nayagarh is a new district carved out of Puri in 1993 during a major district reorganisation process in the State. The process increased the number of districts of the State from 13 to 30. Puri was divided into Puri, Khordha and Nayagarh. As a part of erstwhile Puri district Nayagarh enjoyed the taste of ancient cultural heritage of Puri dating back from 3rd century B.C. The old district Puri lies between 190 28‘ and 200 35‘N latitude and 840 29‘ and 860 25‘E longitude. The new district of Nayagarh lies between 200 5‘ to 200 10‘N latitude and 850 5‘ to 850 10‘E longitude. It is bounded by districts of Angul and Cuttack in north west Kandhamal in West, Ganjam in South and Khordha in the East having a geographical cover area of 4,242 sqm(3,94,110 ha). Major portion of the district is covered with hilly terrain and high land dense forest.

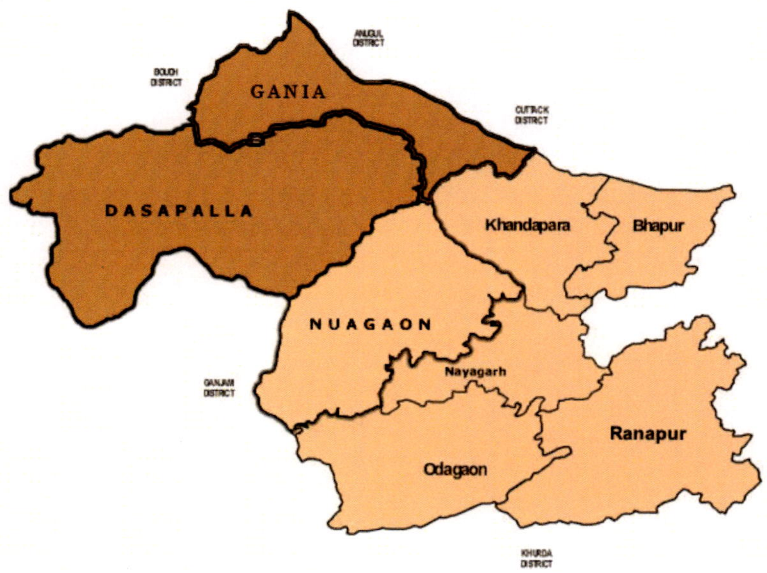

Map 4.4.1: *Nayagarh district map*

(Source : Govt. of Odisha)

4.4.1 Demography of Nayagarh District

In 2011 census the total population of the district was found to be 9,62,789 having male population 5,02,636 and female 4,60,153. The decadal growth rate (2001-11) was 11.37 percent which was higher than the growth rate percentage of the previous decade. The density of the population per sq km increased to 248 from 222. The percentage of the district population to the state population was 2.29%. The sex ratio 5657 decreased from 938 to 915. Similarly child sex ratio decreases to 855 from 904. In 2011 the average literacy was 80.42% which was in the previous decade 70.52%. The male literacy increased from 82.66% to 88.16. One notable thing of the 2011 census data was that there was visible increase in the women literacy in the district as it changed from 57.64% to 72.05%.

4.4.2 Climate of Nayagarh district

The Nayagarh district has two distinct zones. The coastal plain and the hills tracts. The deltaic zone enjoy equitable temperature all over the 3536 year. In the inland hilly tracts, the climate is comparatively drier with highest temperature in the hot months and a slightly cooler winter. From December to February the cold season occurs followed by March to May as the summer. Then from June to September is the monsoon followed by post monsoon October and November. The climate of Nayagarh district is characterized by hot summer and

high humidity all the year around and good seasonal rainfall. The mean maximum daily temperature rises to 440C during May and falls to 100C during December. The maximum temperature is experienced during the month of May.

4.4.3 Agriculture Scenario of Nayagarh District

Agriculture is the mainstay of the people of the district. About 50 per cent of the total population of Nayagarh district depend on agriculture. Paddy is the principal crop followed by pulses and oil seeds. The district also raises sugarcane, maize and vegetables. The total net sown area of the district was 1,33,540 hectares during 2012-13, out of which 51,140 hectares were irrigated and the remaining 82,400 hectares had to depend on rainfall

Table 4.3: Land distribution of Nayagarh District

1.	Geographical Area	3,89,000 ha
2.	Forest Area	2,08,000 ha
3.	Misc. Trees & Grooves	6,000 ha
4.	Permanent Pasture	4,000 ha
5.	Cultivable Waste	5,000 ha
6.	Land under Non-agriculture	25,000 ha
7.	Barren and Uncultivable	6000 ha
8.	Current Fallow	13,000 ha

(Source : Govt. of Odisha)

The total land of the district is 3,94,110 hectre of which 1,33,540 ha is cultivated and, 208,000 ha is forest covered. The district is covered with hills and forests. The river Mahanadi flows on the north eastern boundary and the small streams like Kuannia, Budha Budhiani and Dahuka traverse the mid part of the district.

4.4.4 Agro-Ecological Situation of the District

The following characteristics define the district features –

(i) Rainfed upland with red soil
(ii) Rainfed medium land with alluvial soil
(iii) Rainfed low land with alluvial soil
(iv) Irrigated medium land with alluvial soil77
(v) Drought prone hilly terrains
(vi) Flood prone medium and low land
(vii) Water logged areas and water bodies

All the eight blocks are included in rainfed laterite agro-ecological situation. The soil types are laterite, alluvial, red and mixed red and black. The land used pattern indicates that the net sown area is maximum in Ranpur block followed by Nuagaon and Daspalla. Gania block has minimum. Daspalla has maximum fallow land. Area under cultivable waste is maximum in Odagaon block. This shows that the scope for extension of agriculture and allied sector is highest in this block.

Bio-geographically Nayagarh district covers the forest under Nayagarh Division, Khordha Division, Mahanadi Wildlife Division and Kendu Leave Division of Phulbani (Kandhamal).

The Nayagarh Forest Division has 1063.16 sqkm of Forest of which more than 80 percent is reserve forest. Only a small part of the district, i.e., Ranpur forest area comes under Khordha Forest Division.

The Mahanadi Wildlife Division covers Baisipalli Wildlife Sanctuary of 166 sqkms. Phulbani Kendu Leaf Division covers Daspalla, Nuagaon, part of Ranpur range. It indicates that Daspalla, Nuagaon, Gania, Odagaon are highly suitable for small animal rearing and backyard poultry.

4.5 Description of Ranpur Block

Ranpur Block of Nayagarh District in (Odisha) has an area of 502.16 square kilometers. The block boundary latitudes are 20° 3' 53.892"N and longitudes are 85° 20' 58.621"E. Ranpur block is located around 32 Km from the District Headquarters and around 75 kms from State capital. Ranpur block is having population of 150919 of which male and female were 77484 and 73435 respectively as per the latest Census carried out in the year 2011.

Table 4.4: Area, Production and Productivity of major TOP 5 Agricultural and 10 Horticultural Crops of the Block of last year

S.No.	Agri. Commodity	Area (in HA)	Production (in MT)	Productivity (MT/HA)
1	Paddy	17807	38700	2.1
2	Moong	15000	2575	0.25
3	Maize	700	3200	4.4
4	Blackgram	580	3250	4.7
5	Sugarcane	60	4500	15-18

S.No.	Horticulture Commodity	Area (in HA)	Production (in MT)	Productivity (MT/HA)
1	Brinjal	578	9765.8	16.90
3	Cauliflower	379	5412	14.28
4	Tomato	312	5642	18.08
5	Cabbage	243	6688	27.52
6	Okra	182	1702.8	9.36
7	Cowpea	92	1203.45	13.08

S.No.	Horticulture Commodity	Area (in HA)	Production (in MT)	Productivity (MT/HA)
8	Beans	82	345.99	4.22
9	Leafy Vegetables	76	833.43	10.97
10	Pumpkin	48	1208.6	25.18

Table 4.5: General Information of the block and project cluster. (Demographics, household size, members, and details of occupation)

S.No	Parameter	Ranpur Block
1	Total No of Villages.	217
2	Total Population of the Block	150919
3	No. of Male	77484
4	No. of Female	73435
5	Working population in agriculture	18000
6	Total House Holds	33406
7	SC House Holds	12703
8	ST House Holds	6939
9	General House Holds	13764
10	Avg. members per Household	4

Table 4.6: Socio-economic Profile of the block

S.No	Particulars	Ranpur Block
1	Geographical Area (sq km)	509
2	Population (total)	150919
3	Males	77484
4	Females	73425
5	Population (rural)	129054
6	% rural population	85.51
7	%. of Households BPL	43
8	% of Households APL	57
9	Average Landholding size (in ha)	0.75

Table 4.7: Occupational Details of the block

Sl. No.	Parameter	Ranpur Block
1	Total Population	150919
2	Agriculture / Horticulture as a major activity	53414
3	Non-farm activities (shop owners, non-farm labor etc.)	
4.	Salaried jobs	
5.	Livestock rearing as a major activity	3260
6.	Fishery as a major activity	1204
7.	Honeybee (Apiculture) as a major activity	50

4.5.1 Climate and Soil of the block

The general climate of the block is characterized by Hot and Dry summers and cold winters with the seasonal variation in the temperatures being large / small. The block falls under the assured rain fall zone and average rain fall ranging 1355 mm.

Soil types of Ranpur are Red Laterite, sandy loam.

4.6 Description of Farmer Producer Organisations

4.6.1 Gopalpur Farmer Producer Company Limited

Date of establishment : 19 July 2018

No. of members : 503

Share money : Rs. 5,03,000/-

Total turnover : Rs. 1800000/-

Highlights of the FPO

1. The FPO has been supported by International NGO – Tanager which has provided heavy vehicles for transport of farm produce directly from farmers' field to the market. Transport cost is lesser as vehicle is provided by the FPO.
2. Procurement of Govt Paddy seeds for farmers' use.
3. Setting up of Input shop supported by Tanager including seeds, fertilizers, pesticides among other resources. The members of FPO are given priority to buy these resources at cheaper rates.
4. A Target has been set to build two nurseries in two different panchayats.
5. The member farmers have earned 10-15% more profit when compared to non-farmers of same area.
6. More focus on Investment on Horticulture has been planned.

Fig. 4.6.1: Data Collection from the FPO members at Gopalpur

4.6.2 Prakuti Farmer Producer Organisation Pvt Ltd

Date of establishment : 2021

No. of members : 370

Share money : To be provided by FDRVC for 5 years

Total turnover : Rs. 30000(1st year)

Highlights of the FPO

1. The FPO has been set up by ORMAS under CBBO scheme for 3 years.
2. The finance for 5 years will be provided by the FDRVC (Implementing agency).
3. Implementing Agencies are supporting this intervention by setting up Cluster- Based Business Organizations (CBBOs) at the State / Cluster level to form and promote FPOs as per their requirements.
4. CBBOs are entrusted to assist in the implementation of the program as per scheme guidelines and as may be suggested by the NPMA. The CBBOs are entrusted to carry out baseline survey, cluster finalization, value chain study, formation of groups and FPOs and assist in their periodical meetings, registration of FPOs, training and capacity-building, linking these bodies to input suppliers, technology providers and marketplayers.
5. The women farmers of 64 villages have been registered till now.
6. Out of 370 farmers registered at FPO, 37 of them are tenant farmers, 120 of them are marginal farmers, 89 are small farmers, 50 semi-medium farmers, 38 medium farmers and 36 large farmers.

Fig. 4.6.2: Data Collection from the FPO head office at Village- Gopalpur

5

Methods and Approaches for FPO Interpretation

Research methodology is a detailed plan of investigation and the blue print of procedure for carrying out the research. In this chapter, discussion on the methodology has been made to understand the concepts, methods and techniques, which are utilized to design the study, collect information, analyzing data and interpreting the findings for revelation of truth and formulation of theories. The entire chapter has been broken up under following sub-heads for easy understanding:

1. Locale of research
2. Sampling design
3. Pilot study
4. Variables and their measurements
5. Methods of data collection
6. Statistical tools used for analysis of data

5.1 Locale of Research

The present study has been conducted in two Farmer Producer Organisations(FPO) of the state Odisha. Farmer members from Ranpur block in Nayagarh district were selected for conducting the study.

- The characters and the factors under study have been well discernible to this area
- The researcher's close familiarity with respect to area, people, officials and local dialects
- The ample opportunity to generate relevant data due to the close proximity of the area with the research and extension wing of the State Agricultural Universities;
- The highly cooperative and responsive respondents
- The profuse scope to get relevant information regarding perception on management of water resources, application of nutrients, improving soil organic carbon and problems and prospects of practicing conservation agricultural practices

- Experienced, well versed, venturesome, enthusiast and risk bearing farmers
- Scope of establishing a sustainable and profitable farming opportunities in the area.

5.2 Sampling Design

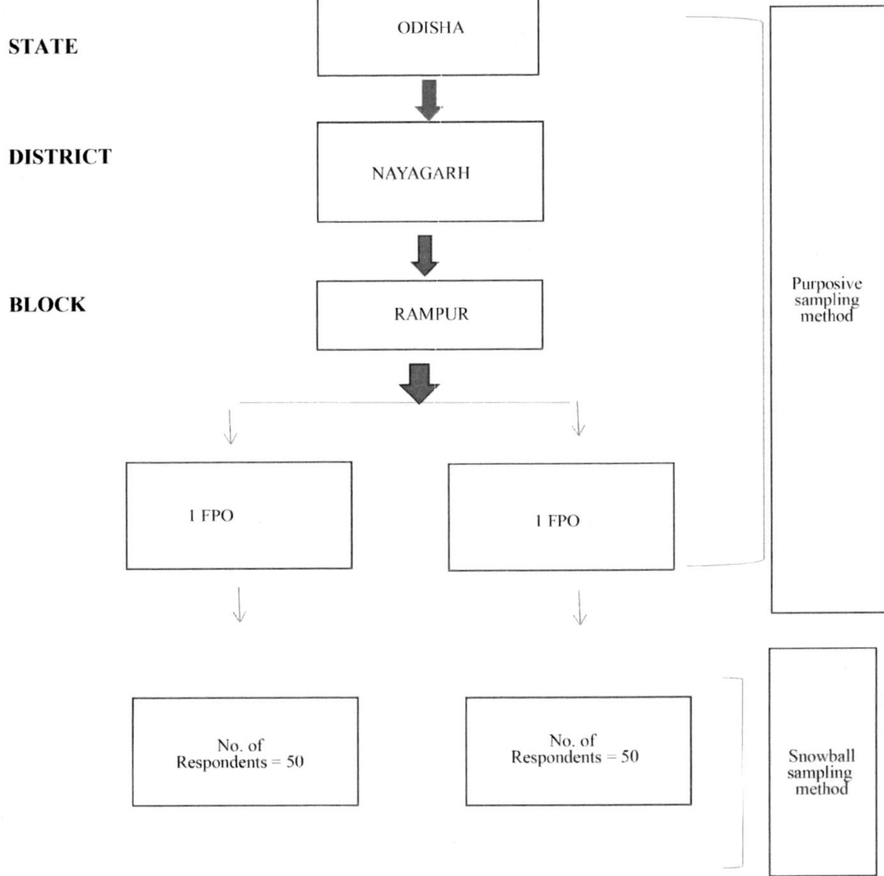

Fig. 5.2.1: Schematic diagram of sampling method followed for the study

Level	Location	Sampling approach	Justification
State (1)	Odisha	Purposive	The home state of the researcher had been selected for convenience in native language interaction.
District(1)	Nayagarh	Purposive	The Nayagarh district has good number of FPOs for which this district has been selected
Block(1)	Ranpur	Purposive	Out of the 8 blocks of Nayagarh district, Ranpur had more number of active FPOs for which it had been purposively selected.

Level	Location	Sampling approach	Justification
FPO(2)		Purposive	2 FPOs had been selected for the study. One FPO was established in the year 2018 and another FPO was established in 2021 which were convenient for comparative study.
Farmers(100)	----	Snowball sampling	For the selection of Farmers, Snowball sampling was adopted as the farmers were more closely related and situated in close vicinity and movement was restricted due to prevailing pandemic conditions.

5.3 Pilot Study

A pilot study has been conducted in the concerned area before constructing the data collecting devices. In course of this survey, informal discussion has been carried out with some farmers, local leaders, extension agencies and state agricultural officials of the localities. An outline of the socio-economic background of the farmers of the concerned villages, their interest in sustainable agricultural practices, experiences of sustainable farming and management strategies against the adversities helped in preparing and finalizing the interview schedule.

5.4 Variables and their measurement

There are two main categories of variables in the present study

a. Independent variables

b. Dependent variables

a. Independent variables

Sl No.	Variables	Empirical measurement
1	Age (x_1)	Chronological age of the respondent (count)
2	Education (x_2)	Year of schooling of the respondent (count)
3	Number of enterprise (x_3)	Number of enterprises one manage in his farm (count)
4	Year of enterprise (x_4)	Number of years associated with the enterprise (count)
5	Training exposure (x_5)	Number of trainings attended till date (count)
6	Family size (x_6)	Total no. of family members (count)
7	Mean family education (x_7)	Total count of educational scores of family members divided by family size
8	Materials possessed (x_8)	By asking the respondents whether they possess T.V., Fridge, Car, etc (count)
9	Size of holding (x_9)	Total area of land owned by a family divided by family size, in acre
10	Size of homestead land (x_{10})	Total area of land surrounding the dwelling house owned by a family divided by family size, in acre
11	Size of cultivated land (x_{11})	Total area of land under cultivation of crop, rearing of livestock, fishery, etc. in acre

Sl No.	Variables	Empirical measurement
12	Size of land under irrigation (x_{12})	Size of irrigated land in acre
13	Number of fragments (x_{13})	Arithmetic count of pieces of the land (fragments) under the ownership of the family.
14	Crop yield (x_{14})	In quintals / year
15	Livestock yield (x_{15})	In litres /month
16	Cropping intensity (x_{16})	(Gross Cropped Area/Net Cropped Area) x100 {in percentage}
17	Income (x_{17})	The income expressed in monetary value generated from an unit area of farm and from off farm pursuits (Rs/capita/year)
18	Family expenditure (x_{18})	Total expenditure incurred in monetary value per month by family members divided by family size
19	Marketable surplus (x_{19})	Assessment over the produce to generate marketable surplus in Rs /month (predicted value)
20	Marketed surplus (x_{20})	Quantity of yield proportionate to total yield as already disposed off to the market in Rs/month (realized value)
21	Family labour (x_{21})	Labour of adult family members equivalent to hired labours per month
22	No of male workers (x_{22})	Number of adult male labours working per month in the Field and their level of interaction
23	No of female workers (x_{23})	Number of adult female labours working per month in the Field and their level of interaction
24	Dependency ratio (x_{24})	No. Of Non-earned members depending on earning members

b. Dependent variables

y_1 = Entrepreneurial information received from cosmopolite sources	
Source	Access(10 point scale rating hypothetically, according to 'z' scale)
Bank, Expert, Institution, Scientists, NGO	By rating in10 point scale

y_2= Entrepreneurial information received from localite sources	
Source	Access (10 point scale rating hypothetically, according to 'z' scale)
Friends, Neighbour, Relatives, Family members, Local leader, Dealer Market	By rating in 10 point scale

y_3= Information seeking and responding behaviour	
a. Come to know	Through self initiative (3)
b. Motivation process	Through peer interaction (2)
c. Adoption process	Through mass media (1)
d. Perceptional process	

y_4 =Entrepreneurial communication behaviour				
a.	Communication flow out	Person	Institution	Frequency
1) 2) 3)	Informed to Advised to Persuaded for adoption	Information given to other persons	Information given to other institutions	Calculating their frequency by multiplying categories of communication flow out process with person and institution
b.	Communication flow in	Person	Institution	Frequency
1) 2) 3)	Received from Advised by Persuaded by	Information given to other persons	Information given to other institutions	Calculating their frequency by multiplying categories of communication flow in process with person and institution
c.	Communicationinteractive	Person	Institution	Frequency
1) 2) 3)	Self mobilization Mutually shared Mobilized bycounterpart	Information given to other persons	Information given to other institutions	Calculating their frequency by multiplying categories of communication interactive process with person and institution.

y_5 =Branding	
Crops and livestocks	Rs/year
Field crops, Vegetables, Fruits, Livestocks, Others	It is expressed in monetary value in Rs/year (also Rs/month)

y_6= Economical Communication			
Source	Volume	Number of visits	Frequency
Bank,	Volume of transactions	Number of times they	Calculating their frequency
Cooperatives,	done	visit the sources	Of visit by multiplying the
Private money			Volume with the number
lenders,Postoffice,			Of visits per year (also per
Others			month)

y_7 = Expenditure for surplus movement			
Mode	Volume disposed	Distance covered	Cost
Truck, Bike, Van, Auto, Cycle, Manual, Others	Amounts end to the market	Distance of the market from the village	Cost incurred for Transportation in Rs/ year (Also, Rs/month)

y_8 = Risk Perception	
Risk typology	**Impact (0-10)**
Financial risk	
Ecological risk	
Technological risk	
Managerial risk	
Weather risk	

5.5 Methods used for data collection

Following methods were used for collecting primary data from the respondents:

a. **Preparation of interview schedule:** Interview schedule was used as the primary tool for data collection. It may be defined as 'a formal list, a category or inventory and it may be added that it is a counting device used in formal and standardized inquiries, the sole purpose of which is aiding the collection of quantitative and qualitative cross sectional data'. Comprehensive and detailed interview schedule consisting of structured as well as open ended questions was developed for collecting relevant information from the respondents.

b. **Pre-testing of interview schedule:** The structured interview schedule was pre tested on a non-sampled area and necessary corrections were made. The interview schedule was finalized after making necessary modification, deletion and addition based on pre testing recommendations.

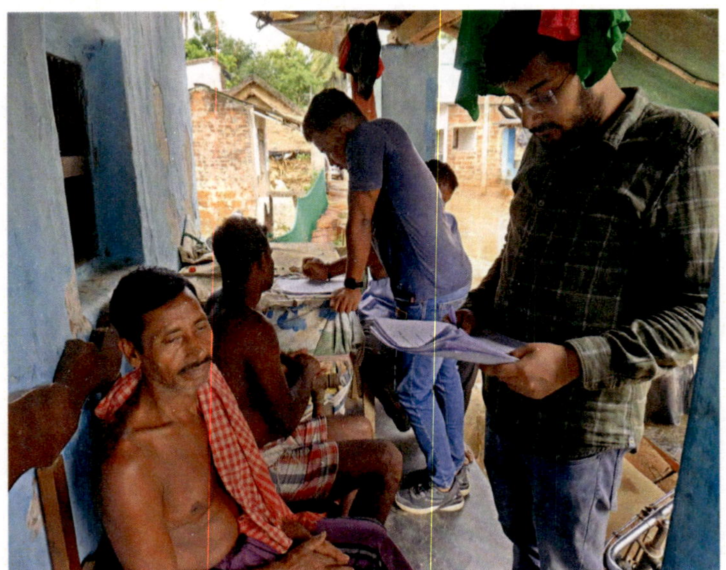

Fig. 5.5.1: Data Collection from the FPO members at Village-Latara

Fig 5.5.2 : Data Collection from the FPO members at Village- Narsinghpur

Fig 5.5.3: Data Collection from the FPO head office at Village- Bimbadharpur

Fig. 5.5.4: Data Collection from the FPO head office at Village- Nihalaprasad

Fig 5.5.5: Data Collection from the FPO head office at Village- Godiapokhari

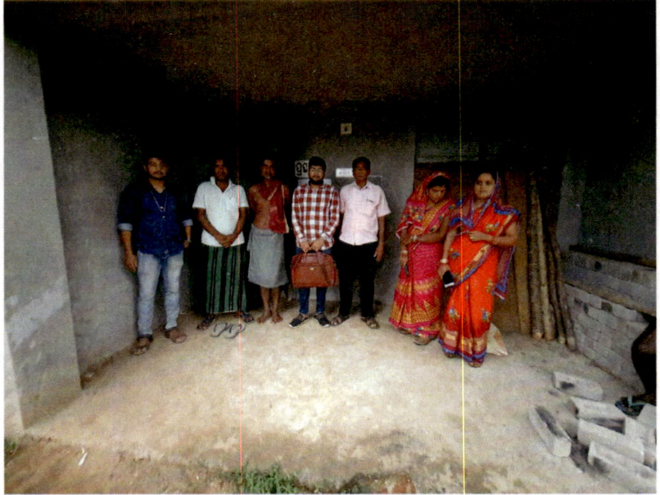

Fig. 5.5.6: Data Collection from the FPO head office at Village- Majhiakhanda

5.6 Statistical Analysis and interpretation of Data (Analytic tools)

The data collected in the interview schedule have been processed and analyzed in accordance with the outline laid down for the purpose at the time of developing the research plan. Processing implies editing, coding, classification and tabulation of collected data. The statistical techniques and tools used in the present study are:

5.6.1 Mean

It is a measure of central tendency (or statistical averages) tells us the point about which items have a tendency to cluster. Such a measure is considered as the most representative figure for the entire mass of data. Measure of central tendency is also known as statistical average. Mean, median and mode are the most popular averages. Mean, also known as arithmetic average, is the most common measure of central tendency and may be defined as the value, which we get by dividing the total of the values of various given items in a series by the total number of items. We can work it out as follows

Mean, $\overline{x} = \frac{\sum x_{ij}}{N}$

Mean is the simplest measurement of central tendency and is a widely used measure. Its chief use consists in summarizing the essential features of a series and in enabling data to be compared. It is a relatively stable measure of central tendency, but it suffers from some limitations of unduly affected by extremes; it may not coincide with actual value of an item in a series, and it may lead to strong impressions, particularly when the item values are not given with the average. However, mean is better than other average, especially in economic and social studies where direct quantitative measurements are possible.

5.6.2 Standard Deviation

Standard deviation is the most widely used measure of dispersion of a series and is commonly denoted by the symbol s (pronounced as sigma). Standard deviation is the square root of the arithmetic mean of the square of deviations, the deviations being measured from the arithmetic mean of distribution. It is less affected by sampling errors and is more stable measure of dispersion. It is worked out as follows,

Standard deviation, $\sigma = \frac{\sqrt{\sum (x - \overline{x})}}{N - 1}$

5.6.3 Coefficient of Variation

A measure of variation which is independent of the unit of measurement is provided by coefficient of variation. Being unit free, this is useful for computation of variability between different populations. The coefficient of variation is standard deviation expressed as percentage of the mean and is measured by the formula,

5.6.4 Coefficient of correlation

When an increase or decrease in one variable is accompanied by an increase or decrease in other variable, the two are said to be correlated and the phenomenon is known as correlation. Correlation coefficient (r) is a measure of the relationship between two variables, which are at the interval or ratio level of measurement and are linearly related. A Spearman's coefficient of correlate

The value of 'r' lies between +1 to -1. Positive values of r indicate that positive correlation between the two variables (i.e. change in both variables takes place in the same direction), whereas negative values of 'r' indicate negative correlation i.e. changes in the two variables taking place in opposite direction. A zero value of 'r' indicates that there is no association between the two variables. When 'r' (+) 1, it indicates perfect positive correlation and when it is (-) 1, it indicates perfect negative correlation, meaning thereby that variations in independent variable (x) explain 100 per cent of the variations in the dependent variable (y). We can also say that for a unit change in independent variable, if there happens to be constant change in the dependent variable in the same direction, the correlation will be termed as perfect positive. But if such change occurs in the opposite direction, the correlation will be termed as perfect negative. The values of 'r' nearer to =1 or -1 indicates high degree of correlation between the two variables.

5.6.5 Stepwise Multiple Regression

Stepwise regression is a variation of multiple regressions which provides a means of choosing independent variables that in the best prediction possible with the fewest independent variables. It permits the user to solve a sequence of one or more multiple linear regression problems by stepwise application of the least square method. At each step in the analysis, a variable is added or removed which results in the greatest production of error sum of square (Burroghs corporation, 1975).

According to Drapper and Smith (1981), the method of stepwise multiple regression analysis is to insert variables in turn until the regression equation is satisfactory. The order of insertion is determined by using the partial correlation coefficient as the measure of the importance of variables not yet in the equation.

The program, according to Burrogh's Corporation (1975), first forms a correlation matrix, finds the best predictor (the independent variable having the highest correlation with criterion variable) and performs a regression analysis with this predictor. Then, the second best predictor (independent), and so on. At any given stage, the group of predictors being used is not necessarily the best group of that size (i.e. the particular group of independent variables does not necessarily have the highest multiple correlation with the criterion that any group of this size does). Rather, this group contains the variables that have the highest individual correlation with the criterion.

Stepwise regression is the step-by-step iterative construction of a regression model that involves the selection of independent variables to be used in a final model. It involves adding or removing potential explanatory variables in succession and testing for statistical significance after each iteration. Stepwise regression is a method that iteratively examines the statistical significance of each independent variable in a linear regression model.

The underlying goal of stepwise regression is, through a series of tests (e.g. F-tests, t-tests) to find a set of independent variables that significantly influence the dependent variable. Stepwise regression can be achieved either by trying out one independent variable at a time and including it in the regression model if it is statistically significant or by including all potential independent variables in the model and eliminating those that are not statistically significant. There are three approaches to stepwise regression:

1. **Forward selection-** It begins with no variables in the model, tests each variable as it is added to the model, then keeps those that are deemed most statistically significant—repeating the process until the results are optimal.
2. **Backward elimination-** This starts with a set of independent variables, deleting one at a time, then testing to see if the removed variable is statistically significant.
3. **Bidirectional elimination-** This is a combination of the first two methods that test which variables should be included or excluded.

5.6.6 Path Analysis

The term 'path analysis' was first introduced by the biologist, Sewall Wright in 1934 in connection with decomposing the total correlation between any two variables in a causal system. The technique of path analysis is based on a series of multiple regression analysis with the added assumption of causal relationship between independent and dependent variables. Path analysis makes use of standardized partial regression coefficient (known as beta weights) as effect coefficients. In linear additive effects are assumed, and then through path analysis a simple set of equations can be built up showing how each variable depends on preceding variables. The main principle of path analysis is that any correlation coefficient between two variables, or a gross or overall measure of empirical relationship can be decomposed into a series of paths: separate paths of influence leading through chronologically intermediate variable to which both the correlated variables have linked.

The merit of path analysis in comparison to correlation analysis is that it makes possible the assessment of the relative influence of each antecedent or explanatory variable on the consequent or criterion variables by first making explicit the assumptions underlying the causal connections and then by elucidating the indirect effect of the explanatory variables.

5.6.7 Canonical Covariate Analysis

A canonical correlation is the correlation of two canonical variables, one representing a set of independent variables, the other a set of dependent variables. Each set may be considered a latent variable based on measured indicator variables in its set. The canonical correlation is optimized such that the linear correlation between the two latent variables is maximized. Canonical correlation is used for many to many relationships. There may be more than one such linear correlation relating the two set of variables, with each such correlation representing a different dimension by which the independent set of variables is related to the dependent set. The purpose of canonical correlation is to explain the relation of the two sets of variables not to model the individual variables. In addition to asking how strong the relationship is between two latent variables, canonical correlation is useful in determining how many dimensions are needed to account for that relationship. Canonical correlation finds the linear combination of variables that produces the largest correlation with second set of variables.

Canonical correlation is a member of multiple general linear hypothesis (MLGH) family and shares many of assumptions of multiple regression such as linearity of relationship, homoscedasticity (same level of relationship for the full range of data), interval or near interval data, untruncated variables, proper specification of model, lack of high multicollinearity and multivariate normality for purpose of hypothesis testing.

5.6.8 Factor Analysis

Factor analysis is a powerful data reduction technique that allows researchers to investigate concepts that are difficult to directly measure. Factor analysis produces actionable data by distilling a large number of variables into a small number of comprehensible underlying factors. It is used

1. To determine how many variables are required to explain common themes among a given set of variables.
2. To determine the extent to which each variable in the dataset is associated with a common theme or factor.
3. To interpret the dataset's common factors.
4. To determine the extent to which each observed data point represents each theme or factor.

5.6.9 Artificial Neural Network Analysis

ANNs are computing systems inspired by the biological neural network that constitute animal brains. Such systems learn (progressively improve performance on) tasks by considering examples, generally without task specific programming. An ANN is based on a collection of connected units or nodes called artificial neurons (analogous to biological neurons in an animal brain). Each connection (analogous to a synapse) between artificial neurons can transmit a signal from one to another. The artificial neuron that receives the signal can process it and then signal artificial neurons connected to it. In common ANN implementation, the signal at a connection between artificial neurons is a real number, and the output of each artificial neuron is calculated by a non-linear function of the sum of its inputs. Artificial neurons and connections typically have a weight that adjusts as learning proceeds. The weight increases or decreases the strength of the signal at a connection. Artificial neurons may have a threshold such that only if the aggregate signal crosses that threshold is the signal sent. Typically, artificial neurons are organized in layers. Different layers may perform different kind of transformations on their inputs. Signals travel from the first (input), to the last (output) layer, possibly after traversing the layers multiple times. The original goal of the ANN approach was to solve problems in the same way that a human brain would. Over time, attention focused on matching specific mental abilities, leading to deviations from biology. ANNs have been used on a variety of tasks, including computer vision, speech recognition, machine translation, social network filtering, playing board and video games and medical diagnosis.

6

A Case Study on "Entrepreneurial Behaviour of Farmers in Farmer Producer Organizations (FPO)"

Chapter Starts from Next Page.

Table 6.1: Descriptive Statistics of Variable with respect to Minimum, Maximum, Range, Mean, Standard Deviation of Values, Variance, and Coefficient of Variance

Variable	Minimum	Maximum	Mean	Std. Deviation	Variance	CV (%)
Age (x_1)	25.000	80.000	49.830	13.954	194.708	28.003
Education (x_2)	0.000	12.000	7.650	3.043	9.260	39.778
Number of enterprise (x_3)	2.000	9.000	3.820	1.388	1.927	36.338
Year of enterprise (x_4)	3.000	60.000	20.180	14.392	207.139	71.320
Training exposure (x_5)	0.000	5.000	2.740	1.419	2.013	51.775
Family size (x_6)	2.000	13.000	4.740	1.502	2.255	31.680
Mean family education (x_7)	1.670	16.000	7.369	2.847	8.105	38.636
Materials possessed (x_8)	1.000	8.000	3.070	1.018	1.035	33.146
Size of holding (x_9)	0.020	10.000	2.415	1.606	2.580	66.507
Size of homestead land (x_{10})	0.050	0.550	0.112	0.061	0.004	54.894
Size of cultivated land (x_{11})	1.000	10.000	2.430	1.592	2.535	65.527
Size of land under irrigation (x_{12})	0.000	10.000	2.095	1.631	2.660	77.851
Number of fragments (x_{13})	1.000	14.000	3.100	2.513	6.313	81.051
Crop yield (x_{14})	10.500	440.000	103.865	94.565	8942.626	91.047
Livestock yield (x_{15})	0.000	150.000	58.400	43.627	1903.273	74.703
Cropping intensity (x_{16})	72.000	235.000	146.025	30.841	951.153	21.120
Income (x_{17})	40000.000	500000.000	143334.570	94889.390	9003996260.692	66.201
Family expenditure (x_{18})	4000.000	30000.000	11355.000	4604.178	21198459.596	40.548
Marketable surplus (x_{19})	2000.000	169624.000	35582.320	22694.166	515025174.139	63.779
Marketed surplus (x_{20})	14755.000	790233.000	181083.990	116518.705	13576608699.081	64.345
Family labour (x_{21})	1.000	4.000	1.630	0.747	0.559	45.856
No of male workers (x_{22})	0.000	15.000	3.150	2.709	7.341	86.013
No of female workers (x_{23})	0.000	25.000	3.950	3.520	12.391	89.118
Dependency ratio (x_{24})	0.200	2.000	0.479	0.282	0.079	58.817

Variable	Minimum	Maximum	Mean	Std. Deviation	Variance	CV (%)
Entrepreneurial info received from cosmopolite sources (y_1)	1.400	5.600	2.836	0.844	0.712	29.758
Entrepreneurial info received from localite sources (y_2)	1.570	7.280	4.496	1.220	1.489	27.140
Information seeking and responding behaviour (y_3)	4.000	10.000	6.670	1.688	2.850	25.308
Entrepreneurial communication behaviour (y_4)	8.670	127.330	56.972	20.033	401.301	35.162
Branding (y_5)	3.000	5.670	3.645	0.612	0.374	16.787
Economical communication (y_6)	25.200	89.630	51.646	11.666	136.091	22.588
Expenditure for surplus movement (y_7)	12.600	641.510	193.203	121.173	14682.934	62.718
Risk perception (y_8)	2.800	8.000	4.888	0.947	0.897	19.379

Result: Table 6.1 presents the distribution of 24 independent variables (x_1-x_{24}) and 8 independent variables (y_1-y_8) in terms of their range, mean, standard deviation and co-efficient of variance.

Revelation: The distribution pattern of variable, **age**, depicts that the minimum age of the respondents is 25 and maximum is 80. The mean age is 49.830 with S.D 13.954. The Coefficient of variance (CV) is 28.003 per cent which indicates that the distribution pattern of the variable is highly consistent.

The distribution pattern of variable, **education**, depicts that the minimum education of the respondents is 0(illiterate) and maximum is 12 (12th standard). The mean education is 7.650 with S.D 3.043. The Coefficient of variance (CV) is 39.778 per cent which indicates that the distribution pattern of the variable is fairly consistent.

The distribution pattern of variable, **no. of enterprise**, depicts that the minimum number of respondents is 2 and maximum is 9. The mean no. of enterprise is 3.820 with S.D 1.388. The Coefficient of variance (CV) is 36.338 per cent which indicates that the distribution pattern of the variable is fairly consistent.

The distribution pattern of variable, **year of enterprise**, depicts that the minimum year of enterprise is 3 and maximum is 60. The mean year of enterprise is 20.180 with S.D 14.392. The Coefficient of variance (CV) is 71.320 per cent which indicates that the distribution pattern of the variable is inconsistent.

The distribution pattern of variable, **training exposure**, depicts that the minimum training exposure is 0 and maximum is 5. The mean training exposure is 2.740 with S.D 1.419. The Coefficient of variance (CV) is 51.775 per cent which indicates that the distribution pattern of the variable is inconsistent.

The distribution pattern of variable, **family size**, depicts that the minimum family size is 2 and maximum is 13. The mean family size is 4.740 with S.D 1.502. The Coefficient of variance (CV) is 31.680 per cent which indicates that the distribution pattern of the variable is fairly consistent.

The distribution pattern of variable, **mean family education**, depicts that the minimum mean family education is 1.670 and maximum is 16. The mean family education is 7.369 with S.D 2.847. The Coefficient of variance (CV) is 38.636 per cent which indicates that the distribution pattern of the variable is fairly consistent.

The distribution pattern of variable, **materials possessed**, depicts that the minimum materials possessed is 1 and maximum is 8. The mean materials possessed is 3.070 with S.D 1.018. The Coefficient of variance (CV) is 33.146 per cent which indicates that the distribution pattern of the variable is fairly consistent.

The distribution pattern of variable, **size of holding**, depicts that the minimum size of holding is 0.020 and maximum is 10. The mean size of holding is 2.415 with S.D 1.606. The Coefficient of variance (CV) is 66.507 per cent which indicates that the distribution pattern of the variable is inconsistent.

The distribution pattern of variable, **size of homestead land**, depicts that the minimum size of homestead land is 0.050 and maximum is 0.550. The mean size of homestead land is 0.112 with S.D 0.061. The Coefficient of variance (CV) is 54.894 per cent which indicates that the distribution pattern of the variable is inconsistent.

The distribution pattern of variable, **size of cultivated land**, depicts that the minimum size of cultivated land is 1 and maximum is 10. The mean size of holding is 2.430 with S.D 1.592. The Coefficient of variance (CV) is 65.527 per cent which indicates that the distribution pattern of the variable is inconsistent.

The distribution pattern of variable, **size of land under irrigation**, depicts that the minimum size of land under irrigation is 0 and maximum is 10. The mean size of holding is 2.095 with S.D 1.631. The Coefficient of variance (CV) is 77.851 per cent which indicates that the distribution pattern of the variable is inconsistent.

The distribution pattern of variable, **no. of fragments**, depicts that the minimum no. of fragments is 1 and maximum is 14. The mean size of holding is 3.1 with S.D 2.513. The Coefficient of variance (CV) is 81.051 per cent which indicates that the distribution pattern of the variable is inconsistent.

The distribution pattern of variable, **crop yield**, depicts that the minimum crop yield is 10.5 and maximum is 440. The mean size of holding is 103.865 with S.D 94.565. The Coefficient of variance (CV) is 91.047 per cent which indicates that the distribution pattern of the variable is inconsistent.

The distribution pattern of variable, **livestock yield**, depicts that the minimum livestock yield is 0 and maximum is 150. The mean size of holding is 58.4 with S.D 43.627. The Coefficient of variance (CV) is 74.703 per cent which indicates that the distribution pattern of the variable is inconsistent.

The distribution pattern of variable, **cropping intensity**, depicts that the minimum cropping intensity is 72 and maximum is 235. The mean size of holding is 146.025 with S.D 30.841. The Coefficient of variance (CV) is 21.120 per cent which indicates that the distribution pattern of the variable is highly consistent.

The distribution pattern of variable, **income**, depicts that the minimum income is 40000 and maximum is 500000. The mean size of holding is 143334.570 with S.D 94889.390. The Coefficient of variance (CV) is 66.201 per cent which indicates that the distribution pattern of the variable is inconsistent.

The distribution pattern of variable, **family expenditure**, depicts that the minimum family expenditure is 4000 and maximum is 30000. The mean family expenditure is 11355 with S.D 4604.178. The Coefficient of variance (CV) is 40.548 per cent which indicates that the distribution pattern of the variable is fairly consistent.

The distribution pattern of variable, **marketable surplus**, depicts that the minimum cropping intensity is 2000 and maximum is 169624. The mean marketable surplus is 35582.320 with S.D 22694.166. The Coefficient of variance (CV) is 63.779 per cent which indicates that the distribution pattern of the variable is inconsistent.

The distribution pattern of variable, **marketed surplus**, depicts that the minimum cropping intensity is 14755 and maximum is 790233. The mean marketed surplus is 181083.99 with S.D 116518.705. The Coefficient of variance (CV) is 64.345 per cent which indicates that the distribution pattern of the variable is inconsistent.

The distribution pattern of variable, **family labour**, depicts that the minimum family labour is 1 and maximum is 4. The mean family labour is 1.630 with S.D 0.747. The Coefficient of variance (CV) is 45.856 per cent which indicates that the distribution pattern of the variable is fairly consistent.

The distribution pattern of variable, **no. of male workers**, depicts that the minimum no. of male workers is 0 and maximum is 15. The mean no. of male workers is 3.150 with S.D 2.709. The Coefficient of variance (CV) is 86.013 per cent which indicates that the distribution pattern of the variable is inconsistent.

The distribution pattern of variable, **no. of female workers**, depicts that the minimum no. of female workers is 0 and maximum is 25. The mean no. of female workers is 3.950 with S.D 3.520. The Coefficient of variance (CV) is 89.118 per cent which indicates that the distribution pattern of the variable is inconsistent.

The distribution pattern of variable, **no. of female workers**, depicts that the minimum no. of female workers is 0 and maximum is 25. The mean no. of female workers is 3.950 with S.D 3.520. The Coefficient of variance (CV) is 89.118 per cent which indicates that the distribution pattern of the variable is inconsistent.

The distribution pattern of variable, **dependency ratio**, depicts that the minimum dependency ratio is 0.2 and maximum is 2. The mean dependency ratio is 0.479 with S.D 0.282. The Coefficient of variance (CV) is 58.817 per cent which indicates that the distribution pattern of the variable is inconsistent.

The distribution pattern of variable, **entrepreneurial information received from cosmopolite sources**, depicts that the minimum entrepreneurial information received from cosmopolite sources is 1.4 and maximum is 5.6. The mean entrepreneurial information received from cosmopolite sourcesis2.836 with S.D 0.844. The Coefficient of variance (CV) is 29.758 per cent which indicates that the distribution pattern of the variable is highly consistent.

The distribution pattern of variable, **entrepreneurial information received from localite sources**, depicts that the minimum entrepreneurial information received from localitesourcesis1.570 and maximum is 7.280. The mean entrepreneurial information received from localite sources is 4.496 with S.D 1.220. The Coefficient of variance (CV) is 27.140 per cent which indicates that the distribution pattern of the variable is highly consistent.

The distribution pattern of variable, **information seeking and responding behaviour**, depicts that the minimum information seeking and responding behaviour is 4 and maximum is 10. The mean information seeking and responding behaviour is 6.670 with S.D 1.688. The Coefficient of variance (CV) is 25.308 per cent which indicates that the distribution pattern of the variable is highly consistent.

The distribution pattern of variable, **entrepreneurial communication behaviour**, depicts that the minimum entrepreneurial communication behaviour is 8.670 and maximum is 127.330. The mean entrepreneurial communication behaviour is 56.972 with S.D 20.033. The Coefficient of variance (CV) is 35.162 per cent which indicates that the distribution pattern of the variable is fairly consistent.

The distribution pattern of variable, **potential of branding**, depicts that the minimum brandingis3 and maximum is 5.670. The mean branding is 3.645 with S.D 0.612. The Coefficient of variance (CV) is 16.787 per cent which indicates that the distribution pattern of the variable is highly consistent.

The distribution pattern of variable, **economical communication**, depicts that the minimum economical communicationis25.2 and maximum is 89.630. The mean economical communicationis51.646 with S.D 11.666. The Coefficient of variance (CV) is 22.588 per cent which indicates that the distribution pattern of the variable is highly consistent.

The distribution pattern of variable, **expenditure for surplus movement**, depicts that the minimum expenditure for surplus movementis12.6 and maximum is 641.510. The mean expenditure for surplus movementis193.203 with S.D 121.173. The Coefficient of variance (CV) is 62.718 per cent which indicates that the distribution pattern of the variable is inconsistent.

The distribution pattern of variable, **risk perception**, depicts that the minimum risk perceptionis2.8 and maximum is 8. The mean risk perceptionis4.888 with S.D 0.947. The Coefficient of variance (CV) is 19.379 per cent which indicates that the distribution pattern of the variable is highly consistent.

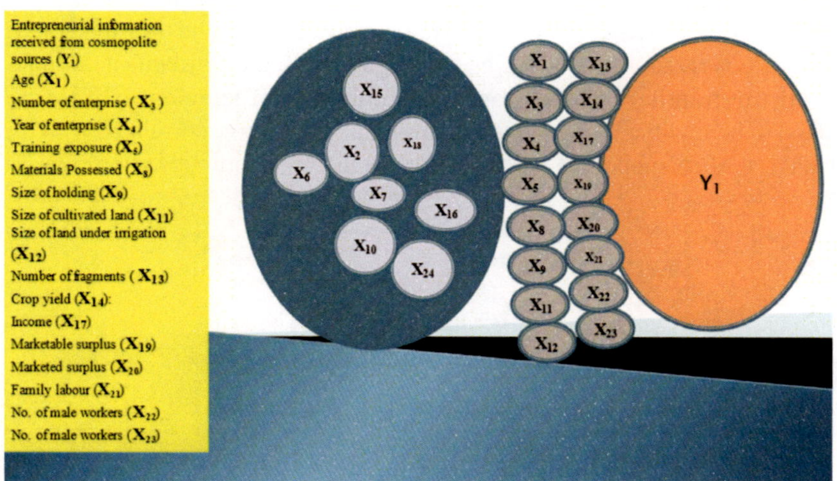

Model 6.1: Coefficient of Correlation between Entrepreneurial information received from cosmopolite sources (y1) versus 24 Independent variables (x1 to x24) related to the FPO members

**Correlation is significant at the 0.01 level

*Correlation is significant at the 0.05 level

Result: Model 6.1 presents the coefficient of correlation between entrepreneurial information received from cosmopolite sources vs 24 independent variables.

Revelation: The variable **age** has recorded the negative and significant correlation with **entrepreneurial information received from cosmopolite sources.** It implies that younger respondents are accessing higher and cosmopolite information sources. It is evincing that more is the **no. of enterprises**, the higher and diverse entrepreneurial information received from cosmopolite sources. Whenever **year of enterprises** have gone up, the entrepreneurial information received from cosmopolite sources has also gone up. So, more experience in year of enterprises have been characterized with higher access to and utilization from entrepreneurial information received from cosmopolite sources. It has also been found that the higher has been the **training exposure**, the more has also been the access to and utilization of entrepreneurial information. High echelon of **material possessed** have also been reflected in higher level of access to information and its utilization. **Larger size of holding, higher size of cultivable land** and **more land under irrigation** have also been dove-tailed to higher access and utilization of information. Whenever the **number of fragments** has gone up, the access to and utilization of entrepreneurial communication and information have also been gone up. This may be due to the fact that a greater number of fragments invites and involves diverse information sources and its utilization. When the **size of land under irrigation** goes up, **cropping intensity** moves up and as a result, it has been found that the access to entrepreneurial information from cosmopolite sources has been escalated. This has also been reflected in the increased crop yield and its association with higher access to entrepreneurial communication and information sources. **Income, marketable surplus, marketed surplus** and **family labour** for their obvious reasons, they have been intrigued with the consequent variable. **Family labour, number of male workers** and **number of female workers** have been found to be involved in the FPO Functioning. These have correlated with the access and use of cosmopolite sources of entrepreneurial communication.

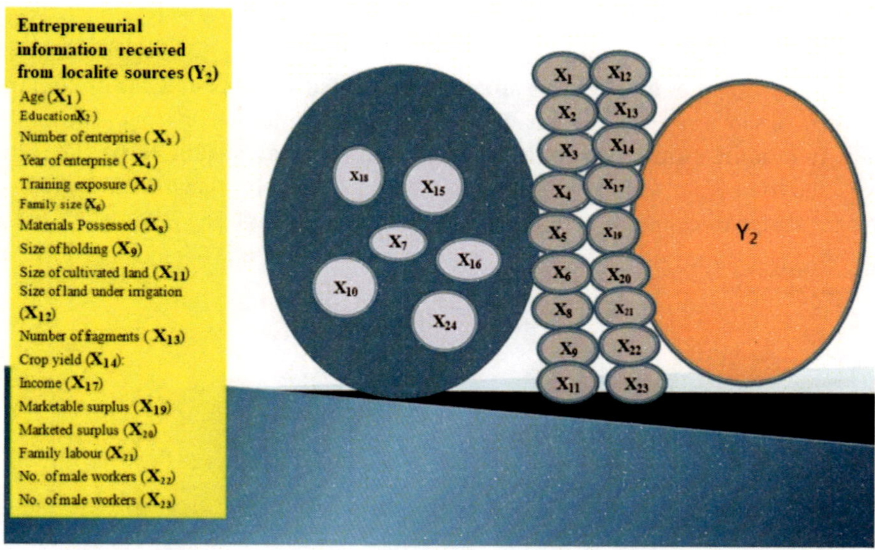

Model 6.2: Entrepreneurial information received from localite sources (y2) Vs. 24 Independent Variables (x1 to x24) related to the FPO members

**Correlation is significant at the 0.01 level

*Correlation is significant at the 0.05 level

Result: Model 6.2 presents the coefficient of correlation between entrepreneurial information received from localite sources vs 24 independent variables.

Revelation: The variable **age** has recorded the negative and significant correlation with **entrepreneurial information received from localite sources.** It implies that younger respondents are accessing higher and cosmopolite information sources. Also, the **education** of farmers plays a significant role as higher the education status of farmers, higher the entrepreneurial information received from localite sources. It is evincing that more is the **no. of enterprises**, the higher and diverse entrepreneurial information received from localite sources. Whenever **year of enterprises** has gone up, the entrepreneurial information received from localite sources has also gone up. So, more experience in year of enterprises have been characterized with higher access to and utilization from entrepreneurial information received from localite sources. The higher has been the **training exposure,** the more has also been the access to and utilization of entrepreneurial information. The **family size** of farmers implied a significant role as more the number of family members more is the number of entrepreneurial information received from localite sources. The high echelon of **material possessed** have also been reflected in higher level of access to information and its utilization. **Larger size of holding, higher size of cultivable land** and **more land under irrigation** have also been dove-tailed to higher access and utilization of information. Whenever **number of fragments** has gone up, the access to and utilization of entrepreneurial communication and information have also been gone up. This may be due to the fact that a greater number of fragments invites and involves diverse information sources and its utilization. **Income, marketable surplus, marketed surplus and family labour** for their obvious reasons, they have been intrigued with the consequent variable. **Family labour, number of male workers and number of female workers** are expected to be involved in the FPO Functioning are all correlated with the access and use of localite sources of entrepreneurial communication.

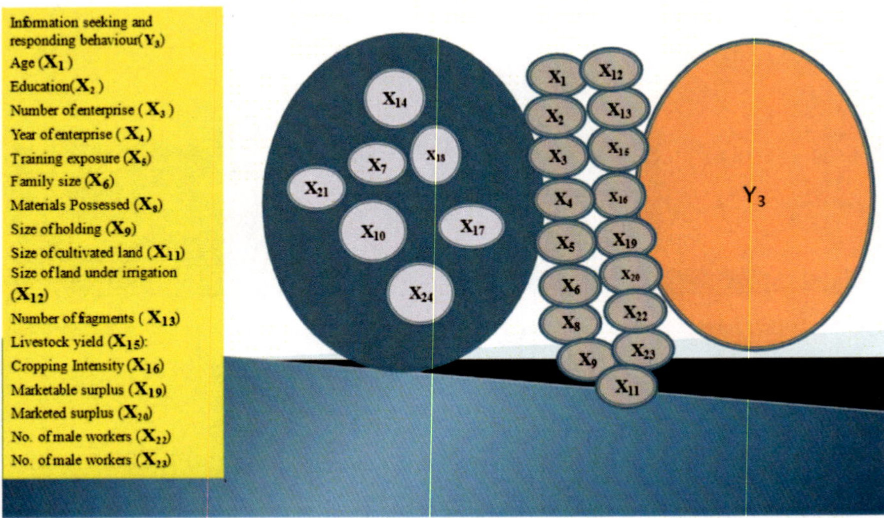

Model 6.3: Coefficient of Correlation between Information seeking and responding behaviour (y3) versus 24 Independent variables (x1 to x24) related to the FPO members

**Correlation is significant at the 0.01 level

*Correlation is significant at the 0.05 level

Result: Model 6.3 presents the coefficient of correlation between information seeking and responding behaviour vs 24 independent variables.

Discussion: The variable **age** has recorded the negative and significant correlation with **information seeking and responding behaviour.** It implies that younger respondents are possessing higher information and seeking behaviour. Also, the **education** of farmers plays a significant role as higher the education status of farmers, higher the information seeking and responding behaviour. It is evincing that more is the **no. of enterprises,** the higher and diverse is the information seeking and responding behaviour. Whenever **year of enterprises** has gone up, the information seeking and responding behaviour has also gone up. So, more experience in year of enterprises have been characterized with higher information seeking and responding behaviour. The higher has been the **training exposure,** the more has also been the information seeking and responding behaviour. This implies that positive results yielded after getting proper training makes the farmer to access more information. The **family size** of farmers implied a significant role as higher the number of family members higher is the information seeking and responding behaviour. The high echelon of **material possessed** have also been reflected in higher level of access to information and its utilization. Larger **size of holding, higher size of cultivable land, more land under irrigation** have also been dove-tailed to higher information seeking and responding behaviour. Whenever **number of fragments** has gone up, the access to and utilization of information seeking and responding behaviour have also been gone up. This may be due to the fact that a greater number of fragments invites and involves higher information seeking and responding behaviour. **Marketable surplus and marketed surplus and** for their obvious reasons, they have been intrigued with the consequent variable. The **number of male workers and number of female workers** have been found expected to be involved in the FPO Functioning are all correlated with the access and use of Information seeking and responding behaviour.

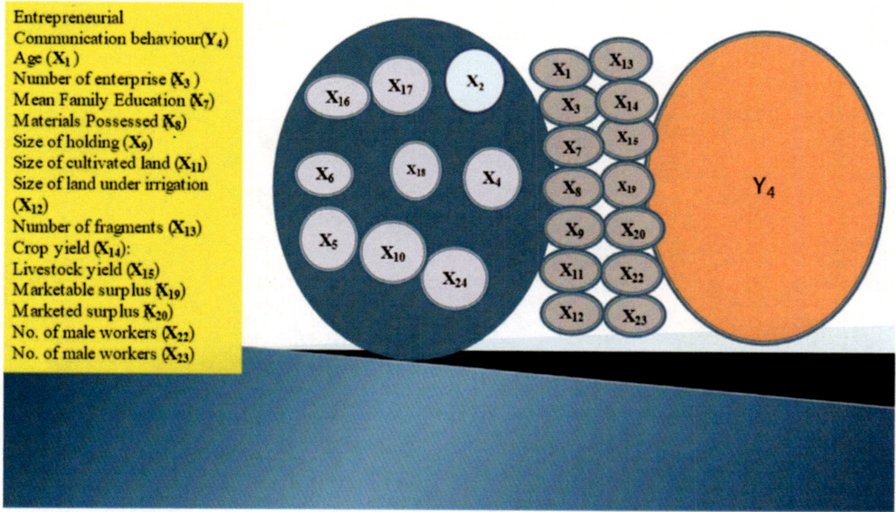

Model 6.4: Coefficient of Correlation between Entrepreneurial Communication behaviour (y4) versus 24 Independent variables (x1 to x24) related to the FPO members

**Correlation is significant at the 0.01 level

*Correlation is significant at the 0.05 level

Result: Model 6.4 presents the coefficient of correlation between **Entrepreneurial Communication behaviour** vs 24 independent variables.

Revelation: The variable **age** has recorded the negative and significant correlation with Entrepreneurial communication behaviour. It implies that younger respondents are possessing higher Entrepreneurial communication behaviour. It is evincing that more the **no. of enterprises,** the higher and diverse the entrepreneurial communication behaviour. **Mean family education** of farmers implied a significant role as higher the education level of family members higher is the Entrepreneurial communication behaviour. The high echelon of **material possessed** have also been reflected in higher level of willingness to access and share information and its utilization. Larger **size of holding, higher size of cultivable land** and **more land under irrigation** have also been dove-tailed to higher Entrepreneurial communication behaviour. Whenever **number of fragments** has gone up, the access to and utilization of Entrepreneurial communication behaviour have also been gone up. This may be due to the fact that a greater number of fragments invites and involves Entrepreneurial communication behaviour. When the **crop yield** and **livestock yield** is higher, it is reflected that the Entrepreneurial communication behaviour is higher. This is due to the fact that when a greater number of information are accessed and shared, it leads to increase in crop yield and livestock yield. The exogenous variables **marketable surplus** and **marketed surplus** for their obvious reasons, they have been intrigued with the consequent variable. The **number of male workers** and **number of female workers** are expected to be involved in the FPO Functioning are all correlated with the access, share and use of information for entrepreneurial communication.

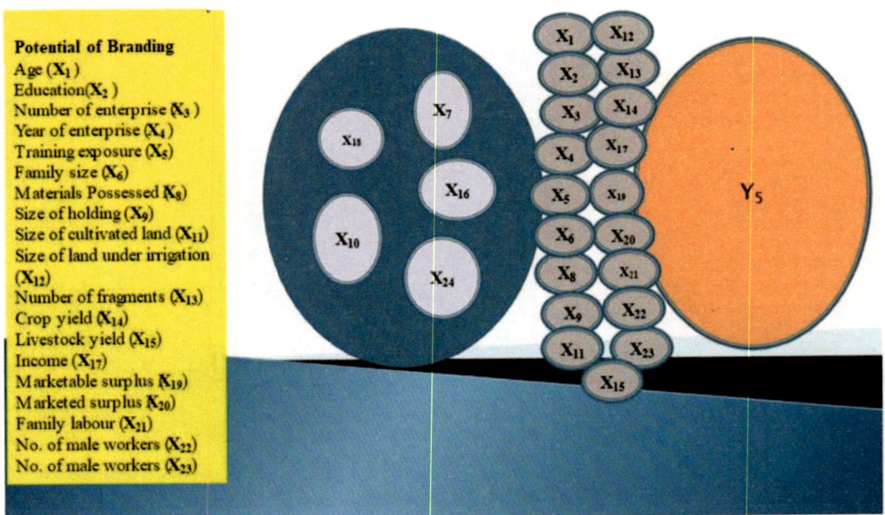

Model 6.5: Coefficient of Correlation between Potential of Branding (y5) versus 24 Independent variables (x1 to x24) related to the FPO members

**Correlation is significant at the 0.01 level

*Correlation is significant at the 0.05 level

Result: Model 6.5 presents the coefficient of correlation between **Potential of Branding** vs 24 independent variables.

Revelation: The variable **age** has recorded the negative and significant correlation with potential of branding. It implies that younger respondents are possessing higher potential of branding. Also, the **education** of farmers plays a significant role as higher the education status of farmers, higher the potential of branding of farm produce. It is evincing that more is the **no. of enterprises,** the higher and diverse potential of branding. Whenever **year of enterprises** has gone up, the potential of branding has also gone up. So, more experience in year of enterprises have been characterized with higher potential of branding. The higher has been the **training exposure,** the more has also been the potential of branding. The **family size** of farmers implied a significant role as higher the number of family members higher is the potential of branding. The high echelon of **material possessed** have also been reflected in higher level of Branding of agricultural produce. It implies that a greater number of materials helps the farmers in increasing brand value of their farm produce. Larger **size of holding, higher size of cultivable land and more land under irrigation** have also been dove-tailed to higher the potential of branding. Whenever the **number of fragments, crop yield and livestock yield** has gone up, the potential of branding has also gone up. This may be due to the fact that more number of fragments leads to more crop yield which increases the brand value of the farm products. **Income, marketable surplus, marketed surplus and family labour** for their obvious reasons, they have been intrigued with the consequent variable. The **number of male workers and number of female workers** are expected to be involved in the FPO Functioning are all correlated with the need and desire to promote branding of their farm produce.

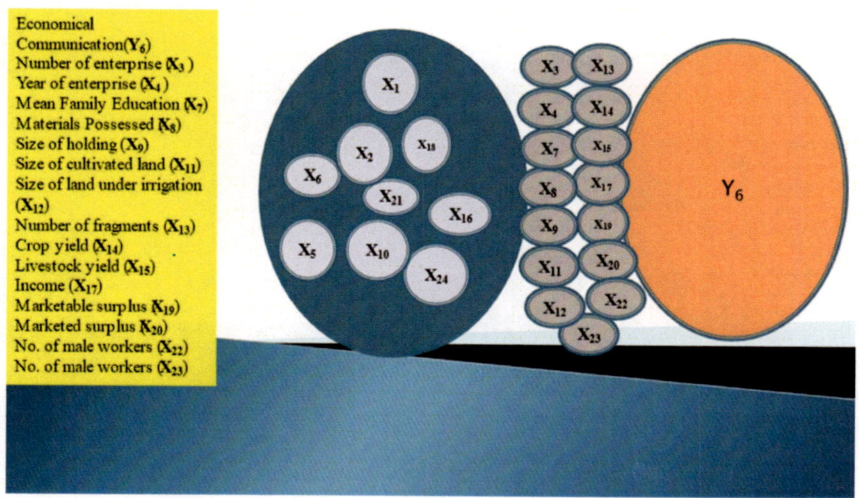

Model 6.6: Coefficient of Correlation between Economical Communication (y6) versus 24 Independent variables (x1 to x24) related to the FPO members

**Correlation is significant at the 0.01 level

*Correlation is significant at the 0.05 level

Result: Model 6.6 presents the coefficient of correlation between **Economical communication** vs 24 independent variables.

Revelation: It is evincing that higher the **number of enterprises,** the higher is the economical communication. Whenever **year of enterprises** has gone up, the Economical communication has also gone up. So, more experience in year of enterprises have been characterized with higher economical communication as financial decisions are taken after much consideration by the experienced farmers. The higher has been the **mean family education,** the more has also been the economical communication. It implies higher rate of literacy leads to more involvement of financial institutions to strengthen farm economy. The high echelon of **material possessed** have also been reflected in higher level of Economical communication. It implies that increase in economical communication leads to increase in possession of materials by the farmers. Larger **holding size, larger cultivable land area,** and more **land under irrigation** have all been linked to stronger economic communication. When the **number of fragments of land, crop yield, and livestock yield** increased, so did economic communication. This may be due to the fact that more financial stability leads to more yield in farm enterprises. **Income, marketable surplus and marketed surplus** for their obvious reasons, they have been intrigued with the consequent variable. The **number of male workers and number of female workers** are expected to be involved in the FPO Functioning are all correlated with the access and use of economical communication.

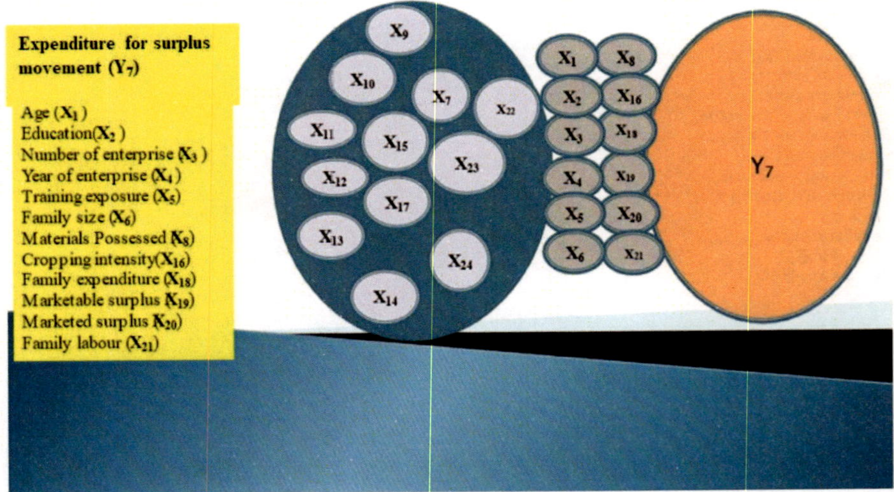

Model 6.7: Coefficient of Correlation between Expenditure for surplus movement (y7) versus 24 Independent variables (x1 to x24) related to the FPO members

**Correlation is significant at the 0.01 level

*Correlation is significant at the 0.05 level

Result: Model 6.7 presents the coefficient of correlation between **Expenditure for surplus movement** vs 24 independent variables.

Revelation: The variable **age** has recorded the positive and significant correlation with **expenditure for surplus movement.** It implies that older the respondents more is the expenditure for surplus movement. Also, **education** of farmers has recorded negative and significant correlation. It implies that higher the education level of farmers, less is the expenditure for surplus movement. It is evincing that more is the **no. of enterprises**, the lesser is the expenditure for surplus movement. Whenever **year of enterprises** has gone up, expenditure for surplus movement has come down. So, more experience in year of enterprises have been characterized with lesser expenditure for surplus movement. The higher has been the **training exposure,** the lesser has also been the expenditure for surplus movement. The **family size** of farmers implied a significant role as higher the number of family members lesser is the cost for surplus movement. When more family members are involved in farm enterprises, lesser is the cost for surplus movement. The large echelon of **material possessed** has also resulted in a lower cost for expenditure for surplus transfer. It suggests that having a greater quantity of materials assists farmers in lowering their expenditure for surplus transportation. The **cropping intensity** has recorded a positive and significant correlation with expenditure for surplus movement. It implies higher is the produce more is the expenditure for surplus movement. **Family expenditure, marketable surplus, marketed surplus and family labour** for their obvious reasons, they have been intrigued with the consequent variable.

Coefficient of Correlation (r): Risk Perception (Y_8) vs. 24 Causal Variables (X_1-X_{24})

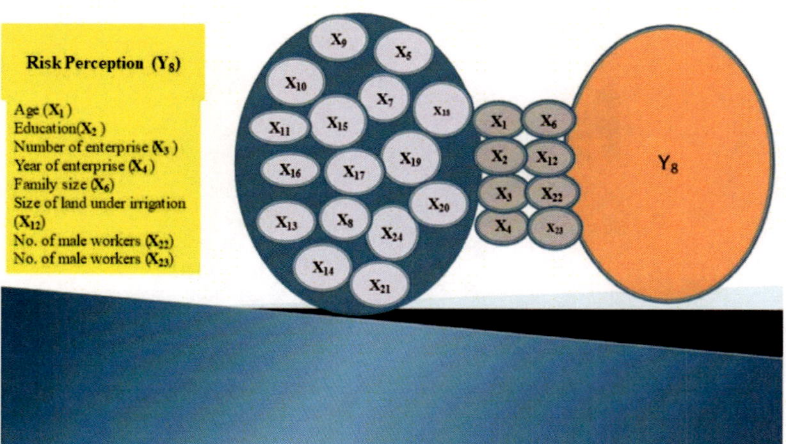

Model 6.8: Coefficient of Correlation between Risk Perception (y8) versus 24 Independent variables (x1 to x24) related to the FPO members

**Correlation is significant at the 0.01 level

*Correlation is significant at the 0.05 level

Result: Model 6.8 presents the coefficient of correlation between Risk perception vs 24 independent variables.

Revelation: The variable **age** has recorded the positive and significant correlation with **Risk perception.** It implies that older respondents are experiencing higher Risk perception and vice-versa. It is discernible that higher is the **education,** the higher is the ability to respond towards risk perception. It is evincing that more is the **no. of enterprises,** the higher is the risk perception. Whenever **year of enterprises** has gone up, the risk perception has also gone up. So, more experience in year of enterprises have been characterized with the ability of farmers to assess the risks associated with their farm enterprise. The higher has been the **family size,** the more is the risk perception of the family members. **Higher land under irrigation** have all been linked to stronger risk perception. The **no. of male workers** and **no. of female worker** are expected to be involved in the FPO Functioning are all correlated with the decision making for the farm enterprise after the assessment of risk perception.

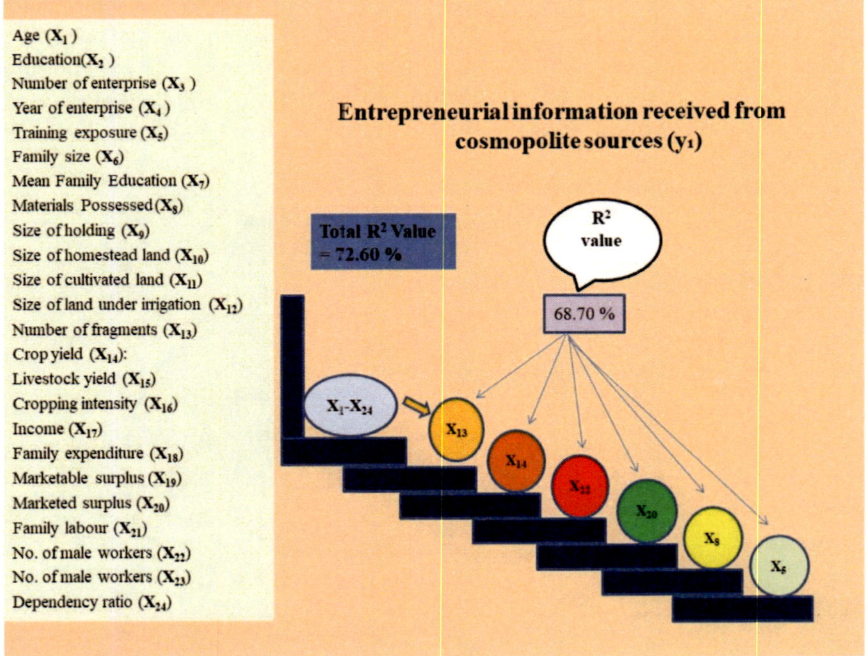

Model 6.9: Stepwise Regression Analysis: Entrepreneurial information received from cosmopolite sources (y1) Vs. 24 Causal Variables (x1 to x24)

R square: 68.70%

The standard error of the estimate: 0.577

Revelation: It is discernible that the 6 exogenous variables - number of fragments, crop yield, number of male workers, marketed surplus, materials possessed and training exposure have been retained at the last step and has substantially contributed to the consequent variable entrepreneurial information received from localite sources. It has been found that **land fragmentation** has also entered into the complex information seeking behaviour. So, it implies that fragmentation is not just physical disintegration of land masses. Beyond that it characterises the behaviour of communication pattern and behaviour disposed of by the FPO members. The socio-ecological behaviour of farmers due to fragmentation of land has had a more psychic effect due to the stress associated with utilization of more labour, resources and time. Fragmentation leads to cost and energy prodigal nature of farmers. When **crop yield** is more, then **marketable surplus** is going to be resulted. When yield is less, market interactions will go down because it is not necessary. Thus, it is contributing to Entrepreneurial information received from cosmopolite sources. The **number of male workers** is more as they contribute to more mobility and exposure to information ultimately leading to increase in **marketed surplus.** It is evincing that materials possessed is more as FPO members are well reckoned due to possession of more materials. The higher the **training exposure,** it leads to increase in knowledge of farmers from cosmopolite sources which again leads to increase in crop yield. This empowers the farmers to increase their income.

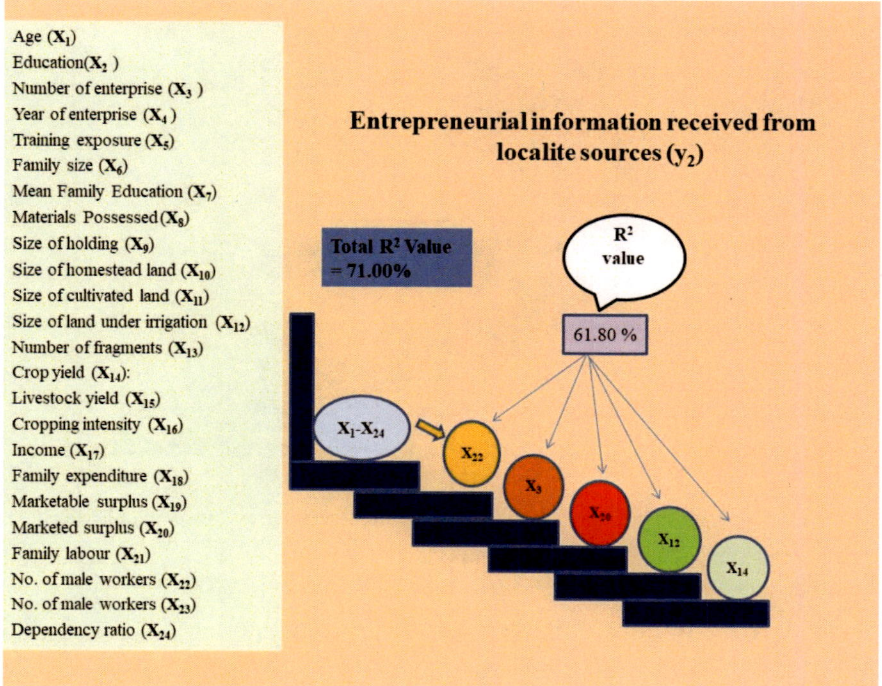

Model 6.10: Stepwise Regression Analysis: Entrepreneurial information received from localite sources (y2) Vs. 24 Causal Variables (x1 to x24)

R square: 61.80%

The standard error of the estimate: 0.634

Revelation: It has been found that the 5 exogenous variables - number of male workers, number of enterprises, marketed surplus, size of land under irrigation and crop yield have been retained at the last step and has substantially contributed to the consequent variable entrepreneurial information received from localite sources. It is discernible that the **no. of male workers** is more as they contribute to more mobility and exposure to information ultimately leading to increase in **marketed surplus.** When is **number of enterprises** is more, then **crop yield** is going to be increased. When yield is less, market interactions will go down because it is not necessary. This is how it is contributing to entrepreneurial information received from localite sources. It is inferred that **size of land under irrigation** is having significant impact as it is possible when various local sources help them in getting the required information and ultimately increase the crop yield.

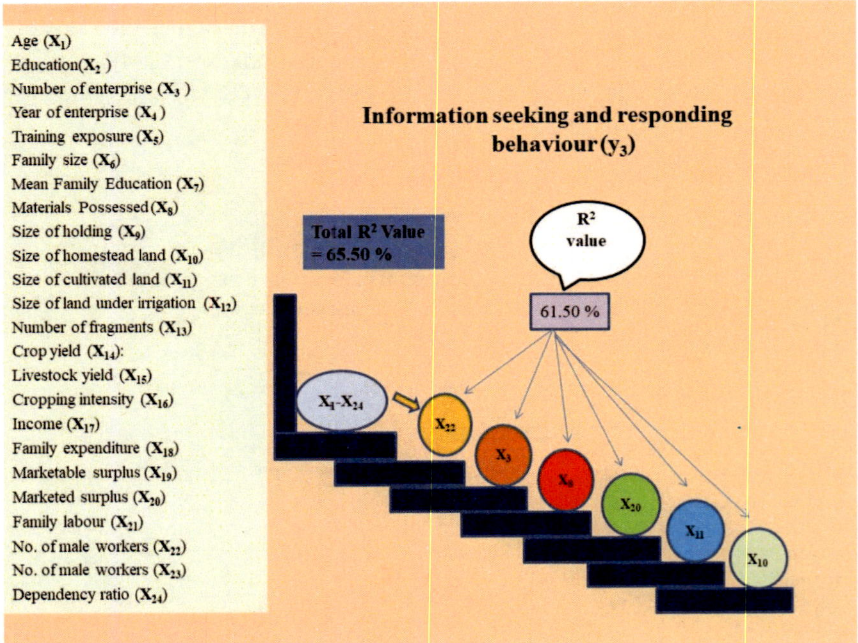

Model 6.11: Stepwise Regression Analysis: Information seeking and responding behaviour (y3) vs. 24 exogenous variables (x1-x24)

R square: 61.50%

The standard error of the estimate: 0.641

Revelation: It has been found that the 6 exogenous variables - number of male workers, number of enterprises, materials possessed, marketed surplus, size of cultivated land and size of homestead land have been retained at the last step and has substantially contributed to the consequent variable information seeking and responding behaviour. When the **no. of male workers** is more, they contribute to more mobility and exposure to information ultimately leading to increase in marketed surplus. When **number of enterprises** is more, then marketable surplus is going to be resulted. When yield is less, market interactions will go down because it is not necessary. This is how it is contributing to information seeking and responding behaviour. When the FPO members have more **materials possessed,** they are well reckoned with to have more information through use of television or radio and be more advanced. The higher the information seeking and responding more will be the **marketed surplus**. The higher the **size of cultivated land,** it leads to higher requirement of knowledge of farmers from various sources which again leads to increase in crop yield. This empowers the farmers to increase their income. The higher the **size of homestead land,** more is the information seeking and responding behaviour of the farmers as it has more potential to provide supplementary income to the farmers.

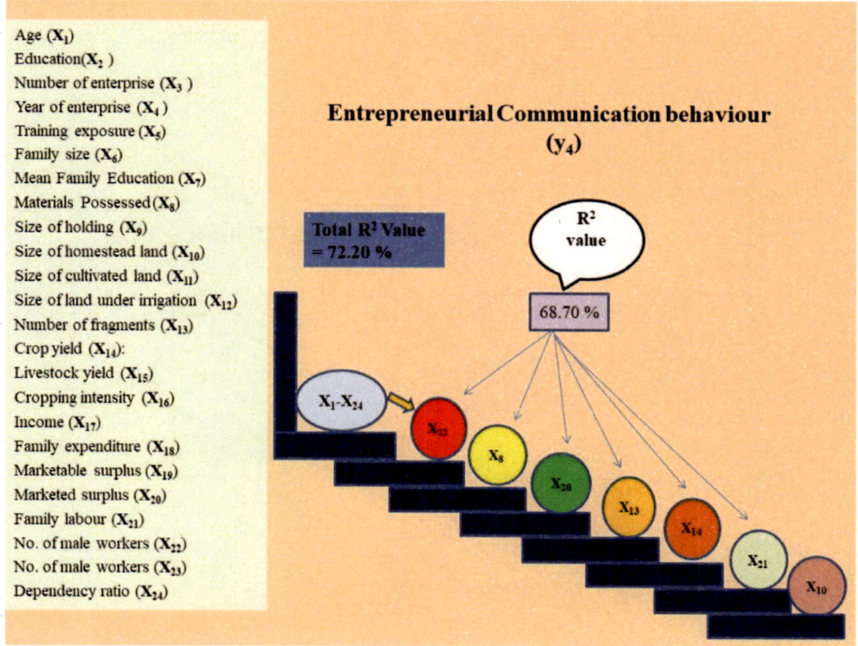

Model 6.12: Stepwise Regression Analysis: Entrepreneurial communication behaviour (y4) vs. 24 exogenous variables (x1-x24)

R square: 68.70%

The standard error of the estimate: 0.580

Revelation: It has been found that the 7 exogenous variables - no. of male workers, materials possessed, marketed surplus, no. of fragments, crop yield family labour and size of homestead land have been retained at the last step and has substantially contributed to the consequent variable entrepreneurial communication behaviour. When the **no. of male workers** is more, they contribute to more mobility and exposure to information ultimately leading to increase in **marketed surplus.** When the FPO members have more **materials possessed,** they are well reckoned with to have more information through use of television or radio and be more advanced. The higher the communication behaviour more will be the **crop yield.** It has been found that **land fragmentation** has also entered into the communication behaviour. So, it implies that fragmentation is not just physical disintegration of land masses. Beyond that it characterises the behaviour of communication pattern and behaviour disposed off by the FPO members. The higher the **size of cultivated land,** it leads to higher requirement of knowledge of farmers from various sources which again leads to increase in crop yield. This empowers the farmers to increase their income. The higher the **size of homestead land,** more is the information seeking and responding behaviour of the farmers as it has more potential to provide supplementary income to the farmers. The higher the involvement of **family labour,** it leads to increase in entrepreneurial communication behaviour as the family members would require the relevant information required for their farm enterprise.

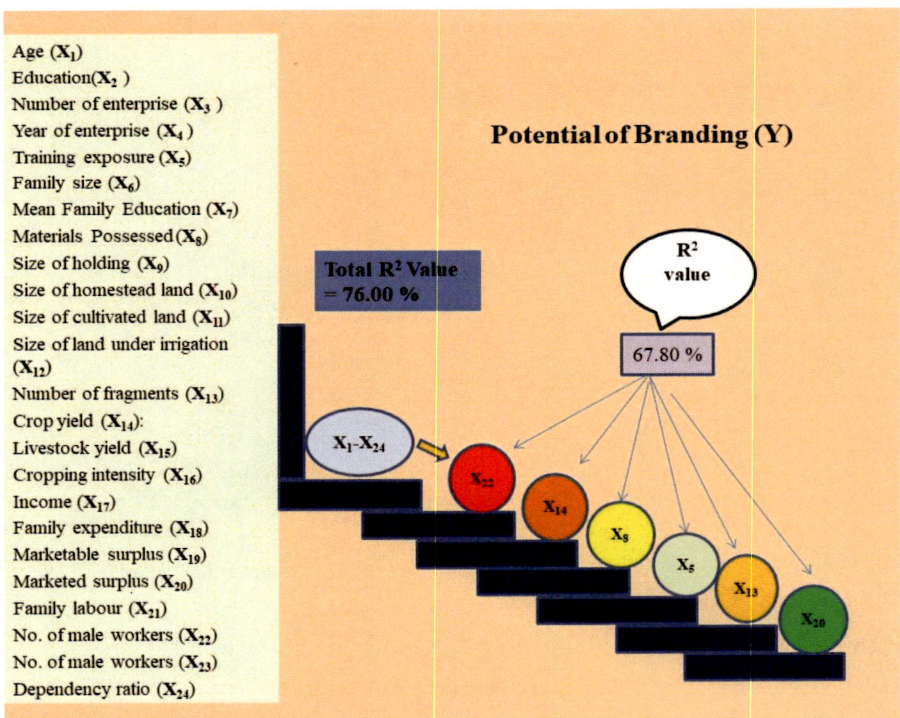

Model 6.13: Stepwise Regression Analysis: Potential of Branding (y5) vs. 24 exogenous variables (x1-x24)

R square: 67.80%

The standard error of the estimate: 0.586

Revelation: It has been found that the 7 exogenous variables - no. of male workers, crop yield, materials possessed, training exposure, no. of fragment and marketed surplus have been retained at the last step and has substantially contributed to the consequent variable potential of branding. When the **no. of male workers** is more, they contribute to more mobility and exposure to new information ultimately leading to increase in branding of farm produce. The higher the **crop yield,** more will be the branding. When the FPO members have more **materials possessed,** they are well reckoned with to have more information through use of television or radio and be more advanced towards branding of the agricultural produce. The higher the **training exposure**, the more will be the branding of the products of FPO. It has been found that **land fragmentation** has also entered into the communication behaviour. So, it implies that fragmentation is not just physical disintegration of land masses. Beyond that it characterizes the behaviour of communication pattern and behaviour disposed of by the FPO members to have a decisive impact on branding of farm produce. The higher the **marketed surplus,** it leads to higher potential of branding of various products.

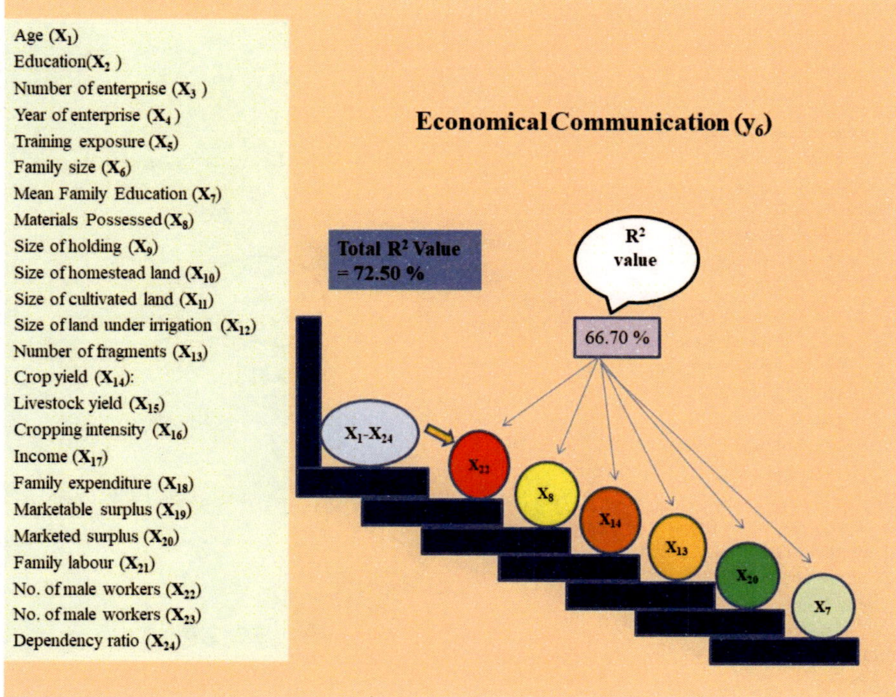

Model 6.14: Stepwise Regression Analysis: Economical Communication (y6) vs. 24 exogenous variables (x1-x24)

R square: 66.70%

The standard error of the estimate: 0.596

Revelation: It has been found that the 6 exogenous variables - no. of male workers, crop yield, materials possessed, number of fragments, marketed surplus and mean family education have been retained at the last step and has substantially contributed to the consequent variable economical communication. When the **no. of male workers** is more, they contribute to more mobility and exposure to new information ultimately leading to increase in branding of farm produce. The higher the **crop yield,** more will be the economical communication. When the FPO members have more **materials possessed,** they are well reckoned with to have more information through use of television or radio and be more advanced towards involvement of economic decisions made for agrarian economy. It has been found that **land fragmentation** has also entered into the economical communication by the farmers. So, it implies that fragmentation is not just physical disintegration of land masses. Beyond that it also characterizes the financial decisions of farmers wherein more land fragments demand use of more money, time and resources. Higher the **marketed surplus,** it leads to requirement of higher investment. Higher the **mean family education,** higher is the interaction of family members towards economic decisions for their farm enterprise.

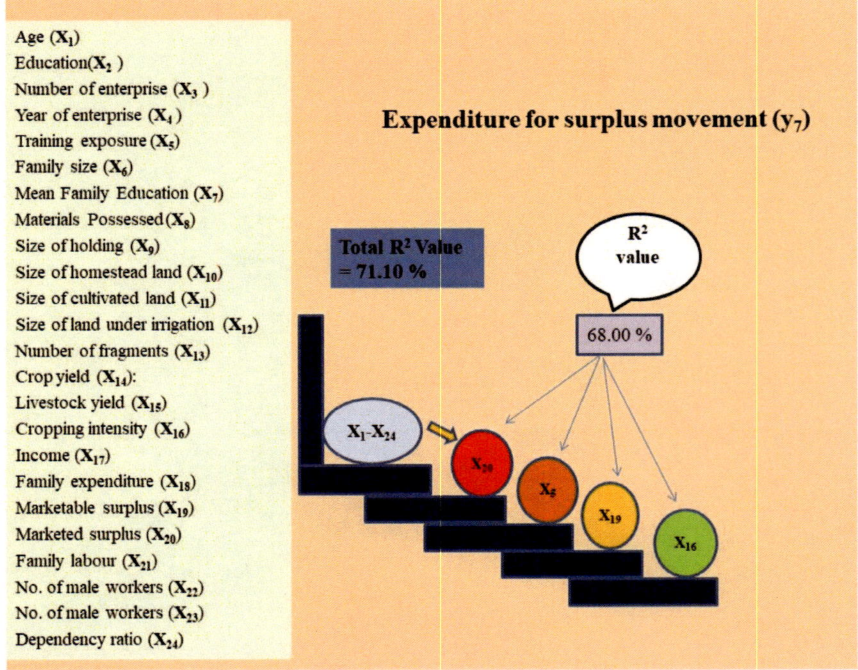

Model 6.15: Stepwise Regression Analysis: Expenditure for surplus movement (y7) vs. 24 exogenous variables (x1-x24)

R square: 68.00%

The standard error of the estimate: 0.577

Revelation: It has been found that the 4 exogenous variables - marketed surplus, training exposure, marketable surplus and cropping intensity have been retained at the last step and has substantially contributed to the consequent variable expenditure for surplus movement. Higher the **marketed surplus,** higher is the expenditure for surplus movement. Higher the **training exposure**, lower is the expenditure cost for marketed surplus. Higher the **marketable surplus,** higher is the expenditure for surplus movement. Higher the **cropping intensity,** more will be the yield. More crop yield leads to higher cost for surplus movement.

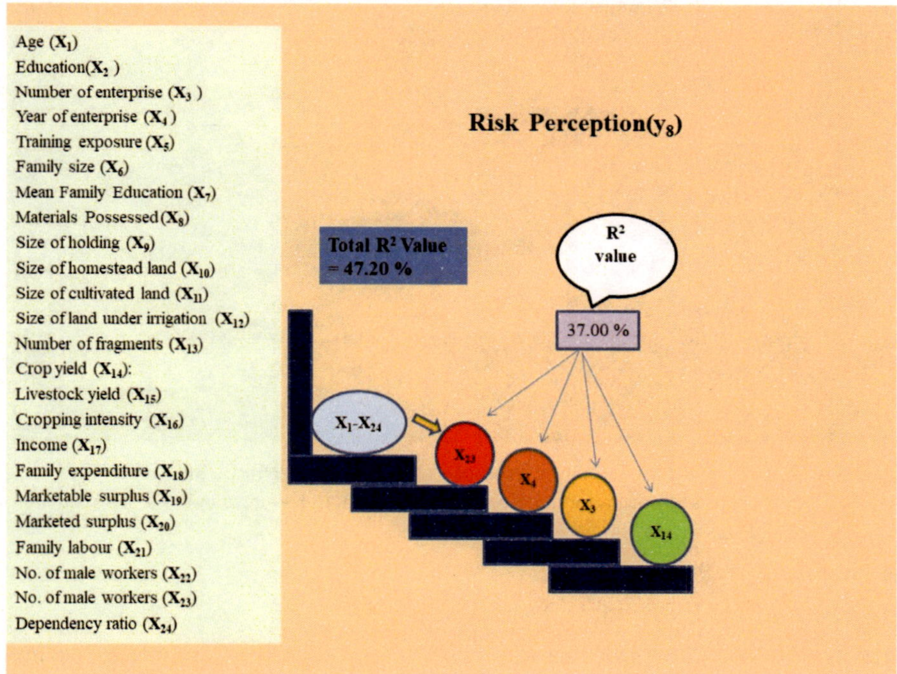

Model 6.16: Stepwise Regression Analysis: Risk perception (y8) vs. 24 exogenous variables (x1-x24)

R square: 37.00%

The standard error of the estimate: 0.810

Revelation: It has been found that the 4 exogenous variables – number of female workers, year of enterprise, number of enterprise and crop yield have been retained at the last step and has substantially contributed to the consequent variable **risk perception.**

- Higher the **number of female workers** higher is the risk perception.
- Higher the **year of enterprise** higher will be the risk perception.

- Higher the **number of enterprise** higher is the risk perception.
- Higher the **crop yield** higher is the risk perception.

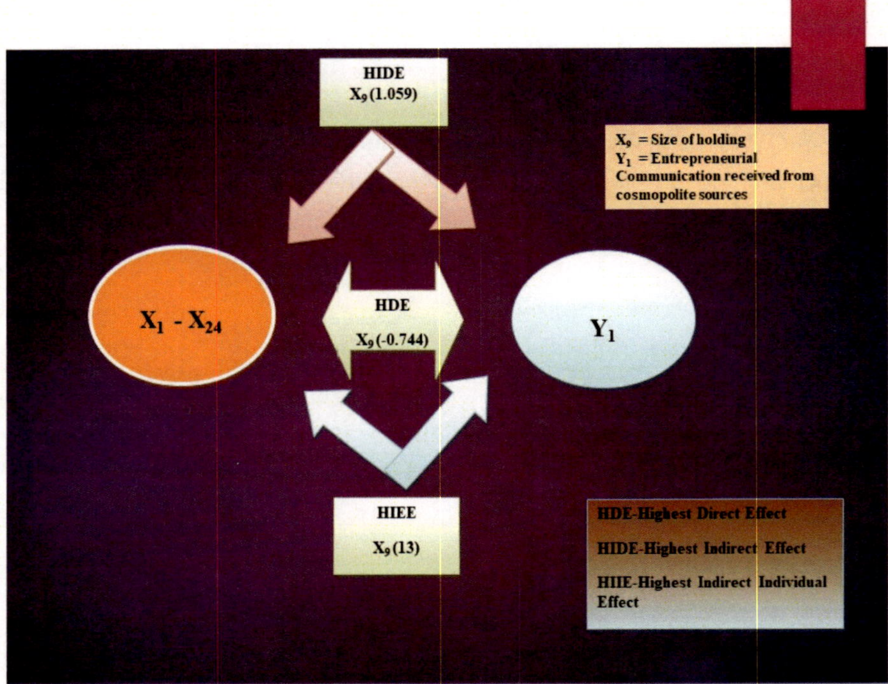

Model 6.17: Path Analysis: Decomposition of Total Effect into Direct, Indirect and Residual Effect: Entrepreneurial information received from cosmopolite sources (y1) vs. 24 exogenous variables (x1-x24)

Residual effect: 0.274

Highest Indirect Individual effect: x_9 (13)

Result: Model 6.17 presents the path analysis by decomposing the total effect into direct, indirect and residual effects.

Revelation: It has been found that the variable **size of holding** has got substantive direct effect on Entrepreneurial information received from cosmopolite sources. Close to it, **size of cultivated land** has also exerted substantive impact, i.e., direct effect on y_1. Land resources have come out as the strongest determinant to characterize the consequent variable. It has got cause and effect relationship. When a farmer is having higher size of holding, propensity towards surplus generating agriculture could go stronger. That is how both these variables have generated substantive effect on entrepreneurial information received from cosmopolite sources. **The number of fragments (x_{13})** has exerted the highest total effect. Fragmentation of land emerging as the strongest determinant to characterize the process of modernization, else it could act as strong barrier to modernization because it will make the fragmentation of land as cost and energy prodigal. The variable **size of holding** has rooted the highest indirect impact of as much as 13 exogenous variables to impact on the consequent variable y_1. The size of holding is characterizing the impact on y_1 in all its forms and approaches like direct and indirect effect. The residual effect being **0.274**, it is to infer that even with the combination of 24 exogenous variables, **27.4 per cent** variance in Entrepreneurial information received from cosmopolite sources cannot be explained.

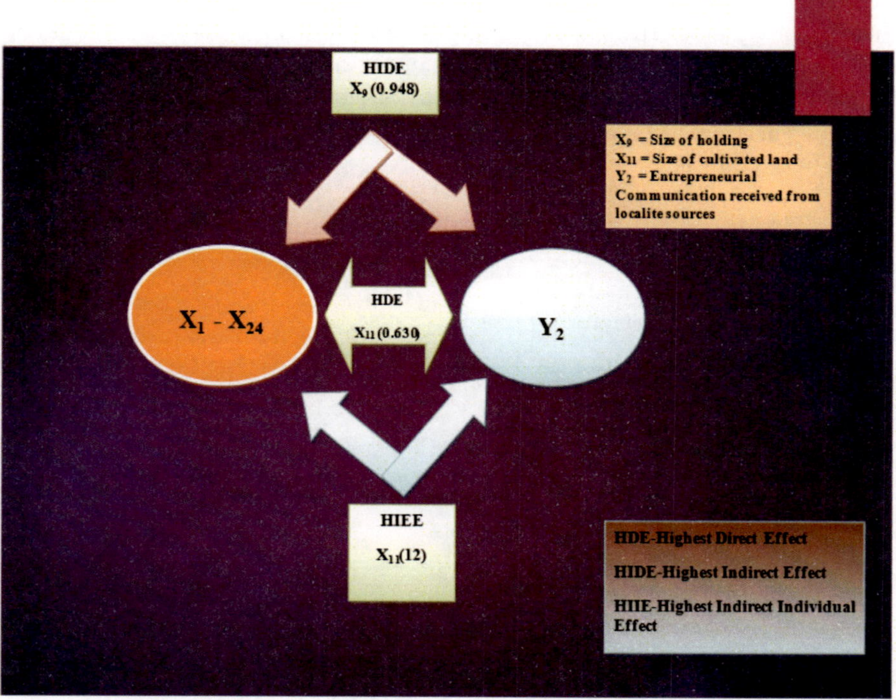

Model 6.18: Path Analysis: Decomposition of Total Effect into Direct, Indirect and Residual Effect: Entrepreneurial information received from localite sources (y2) vs. 24 exogenous variables (x1-x24)

Residual effect: 0.290

Highest Indirect Individual effect: x_{11} (12)

Result: Table 6.18 presents the path analysis by decomposing the total effect into direct, indirect and residual effects.

Revelation: It has been found that the variable **size of cultivated land** has got substantive direct effect on entrepreneurial information received from localite sources. Close to it, **size of holding** has also exerted substantive impact, i.e., direct effect on y_2. Land resources have come out as the strongest determinant to characterise entrepreneurial information received from localite sources. It has got cause and effect relationship. When a farmer is having higher size of holding, with propensity towards surplus generating agriculture could go stronger. That is how both these variables have generated substantive effect on entrepreneurial information received from localite sources. **The number of male workers** has exerted the highest total effect. More number of male workers facilitates the inward flow of Entrepreneurial information received from localite sources due to their high mobility. The exogenous variable **size of cultivated land** has rooted the highest indirect impact of as much as 12 exogenous variables to impact on the consequent variable. The size of holding is characterizing the impact on y_2 in all its forms and approaches like direct and indirect effect. The residual effect being **0.290,** it is to infer that even with the combination of 24 exogenous variables, **29 per cent variance** in Entrepreneurial information received from localite sources cannot be explained.

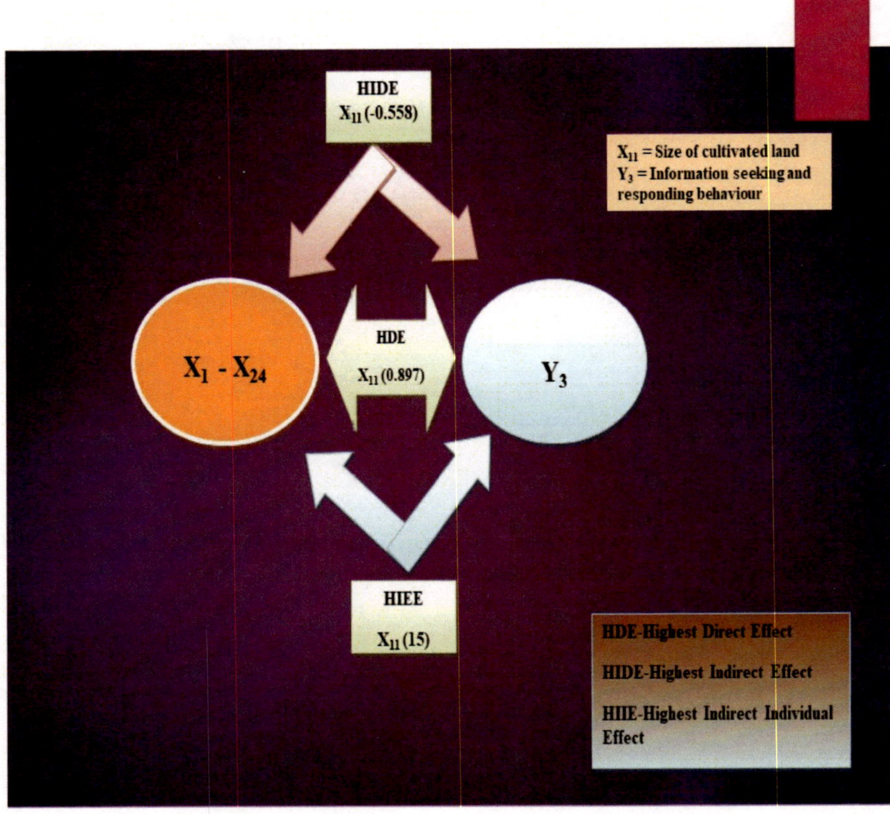

Model 6.19: Path Analysis: Decomposition of Total Effect into Direct, Indirect and Residual Effect: Information seeking and responding behaviour (y3) vs. 24 exogenous variables (x1-x24)

Residual effect: 0.345

Highest Indirect Individual effect: x_{11} (15)

Result: Model 6.19 presents the path analysis by decomposing the total effect into direct, indirect and residual effects.

Revelation: It has been found that the variable **size of cultivated land** has got substantive direct effect on **information seeking and responding behaviour.** It has got cause and effect relationship. When a farmer is having higher size of cultivated land, with propensity towards surplus generating agriculture could go stronger. That is how both these variables have generated substantive effect on y_3. **The number of male workers** has exerted the highest total effect. More number of male workers tends to be exposed to more information unlike female workers especially in rural areas which leads to increase in information seeking and responding behaviour. The exogenous variable **size of cultivated land** has rooted the highest indirect impact of as much as 15 exogenous variables to impact on the consequent variable y3. The size of holding is characterizing the impact on y_3 in all its forms and approaches like direct and indirect effect. The residual effect being **0.345**, it is to infer that even with the combination of 24 exogenous variables, **34.5 per cent variance** in information seeking and responding behaviour cannot be explained.

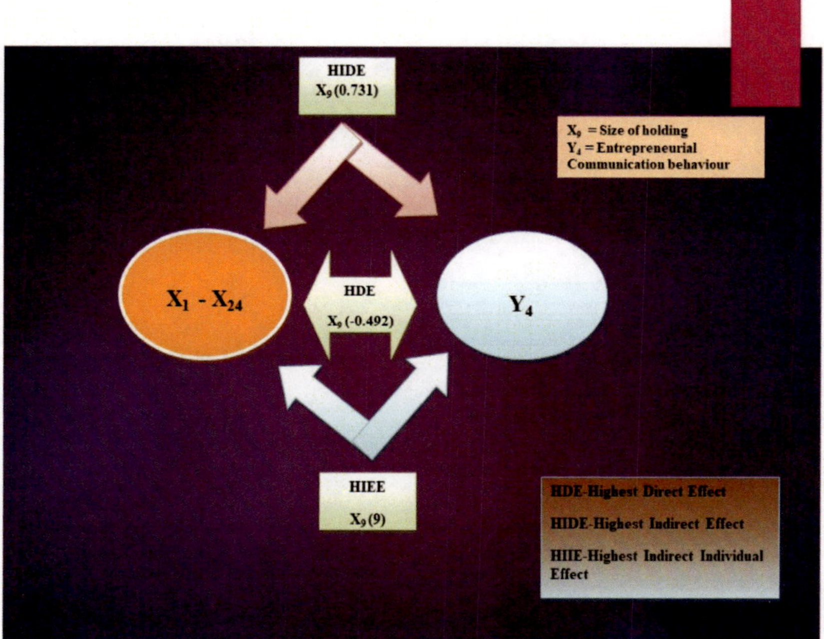

Model 6.20: Path Analysis: Decomposition of Total Effect into Direct, Indirect and Residual Effect: Entrepreneurial communication behaviour (y4) vs. 24 exogenous variables (x1-x24)

Residual effect: 0.279

Highest Indirect Individual effect: x_9 (9)

Result: Model 6.20 presents the path analysis by decomposing the total effect into direct, indirect and residual effects.

Revelation: It has been found that the variable **size of holding** has got substantive direct effect on **entrepreneurial communication behaviour.** Close to it, **number of male workers** has also exerted substantive impact, i.e., direct effect on y_4. It has got cause and effect relationship. When a farmer is having higher size of holding along with stronger manpower, this leads to more production in marketed surplus. That is how both these variables have generated substantive effect on entrepreneurial communication behaviour. **Number of fragments** has exerted the highest total effect. Fragmentation of land has great impact on Communication behaviour of farmers as diversification of land fragments has higher need for proper management and sustainability. The variable **size of holding** has rooted the highest indirect impact of as much as 9 exogenous variables to impact on the consequent variable y_4. The size of holding is characterizing the impact on y_4 in all its forms and approaches like direct and indirect effect. The residual effect being **0.279**, it is to infer that even with the combination of 24 exogenous variables, **27.9 per cent variance** in entrepreneurial communication behaviour cannot be explained.

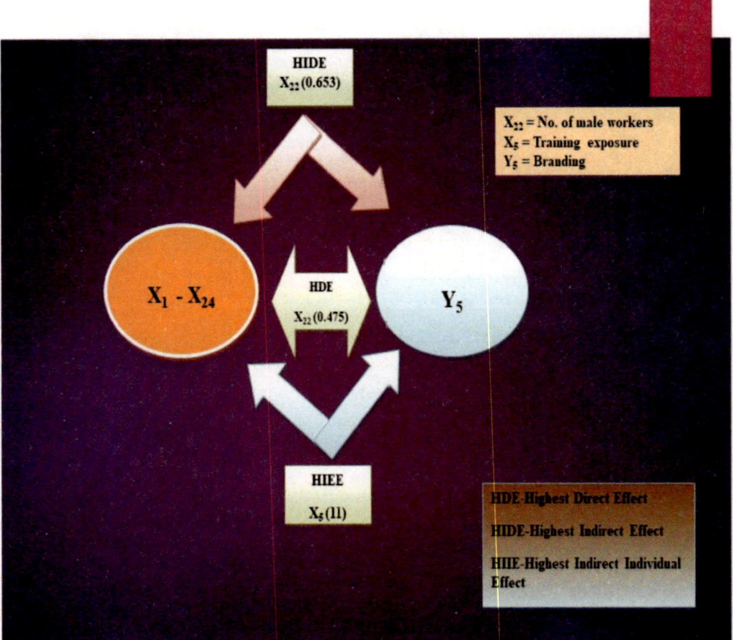

Model 6.21: Path Analysis: Decomposition of Total Effect into Direct, Indirect and Residual Effect: Potential of Branding (y5) vs. 24 exogenous variables (x1-x24)

Residual effect: 0.241

Highest Indirect Individual effect: x_5 (11)

Result: Model 6.21 presents the path analysis by decomposing the total effect into direct, indirect and residual effects.

Revelation: It has been found that the variable number of male workers has got both substantive direct effect and total effect on **potential of branding.** It has got cause and effect relationship. When a farmer is having More training exposure, high mobility as well as higher communication behaviour, branding of products can be done easily. That is how no. of male workers have generated substantive effect on y_5. The exogenous variable **training exposure** has rooted the highest indirect impact of as much as 11 exogenous variables to impact on the consequent variable y_5. It implies that proper training practices helps in knowledge building of farmers and increases branding by the FPO members. The residual effect being **0.241**, it is to infer that even with the combination of 24 exogenous variables, **24.1 per cent variance** in potential of branding cannot be explained.

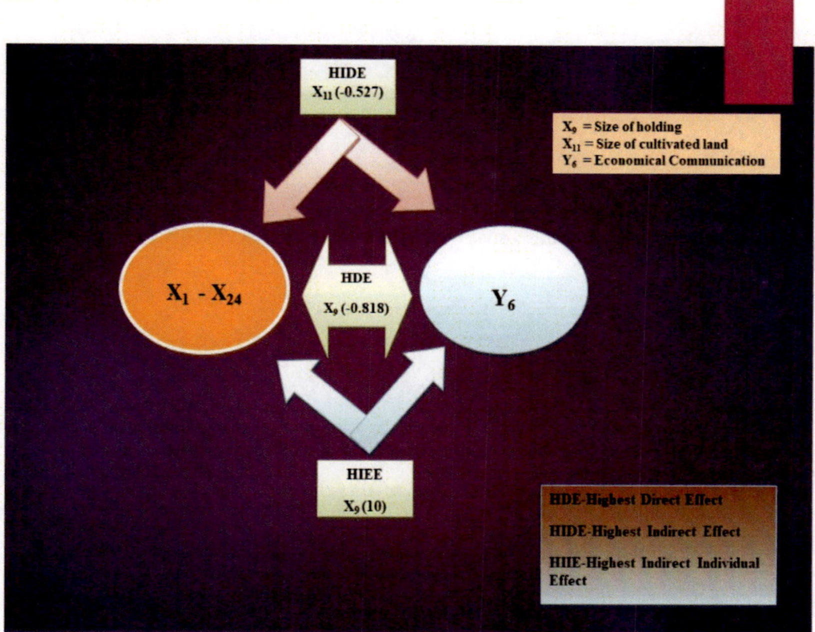

Model 6.22: Path Analysis: Decomposition of Total Effect into Direct, Indirect and Residual Effect: Economical Communication (y6) vs. 24 exogenous variables (x1-x24)

Residual effect: 0.277

Highest Indirect Individual effect: x_9 (10)

Result: Model 6.22 presents the path analysis by decomposing the total effect into direct, indirect and residual effects.

Revelation: It has been found that the variable **size of holding** has got substantive direct effect on **Economical communication.** Close to it, **size of cultivated land** has also exerted substantive impact, i.e., direct effect on y_6. When a farmer is having higher size of holding the cost of production is higher as compared to small and marginal farmers which leads to increase in capital requirement for farm production. That is how both these variables have generated substantive effect on y_6. **The number of male workers** has exerted the highest total effect. It implies that higher information exposure as well as Government schemes facilitates in getting the financial help required for the farm enterprise. The exogenous variable **size of holding** has rooted the highest indirect impact of as much as 10 exogenous variables to impact on the consequent variable y_6. It implies that proper proper economical communication helps the FPO members in taking the suitable financial decisions and increase their income. The residual effect being **0.277**, it is to infer that even with the combination of 24 exogenous variables, **27.7 per cent variance** in economical communication cannot be explained.

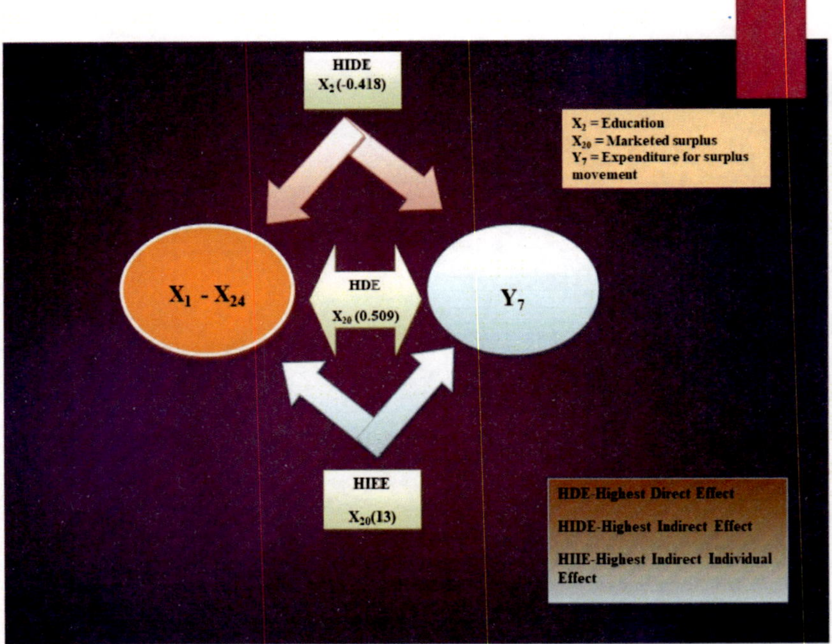

Model 6.23: Path Analysis: Decomposition of Total Effect into Direct, Indirect and Residual Effect: Expenditure for surplus movement (y7) vs. 24 exogenous variables (x1-x24)

Residual effect: 0.290

Highest Indirect Individual effect: x_{20} (13)

Result: Table 6.23 presents the path analysis by decomposing the total effect into direct, indirect and residual effects.

Revelation: It has been found that the exogenous variable **marketed surplus** has got substantive direct effect on **expenditure for surplus movement.** When a farmer is producing higher marketed surplus the cost of transportation is also higher as compared to small and marginal farmers which leads to increase in farm expenditure. The exogenous variable **training exposure** has exerted the highest total effect. It implies that higher information exposure as well Government schemes facilitates in getting the financial help required for the farm enterprise. The exogenous variable **marketed surplus** has rooted the highest indirect impact of as much as 13 exogenous variables to impact on the consequent variable y_7. It implies that more marketed surplus increases the investment of farm enterprise and FPO members have to deal with it to minimize the input cost. The residual effect being **0.290**, it is to infer that even with the combination of 24 exogenous variables, **29 per cent variance** in y_7 (Expenditure for surplus movement) cannot be explained.

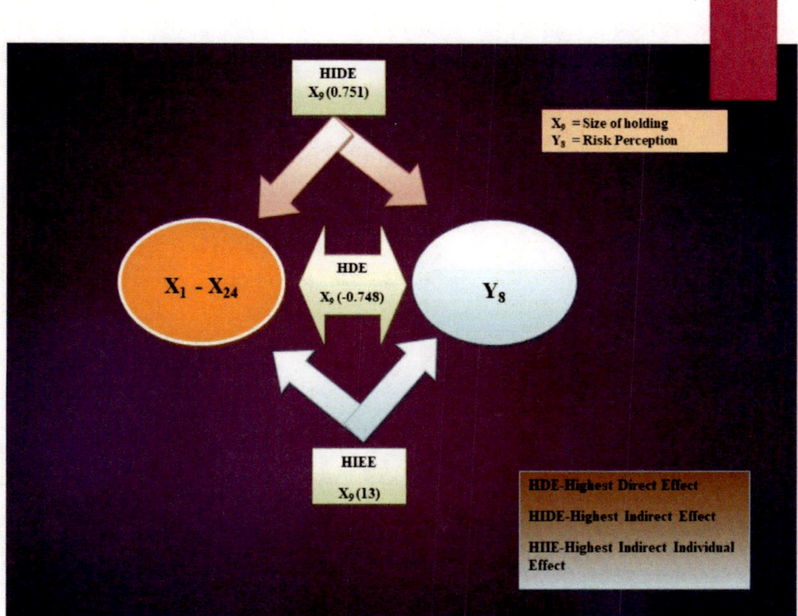

Model 6.24: Path Analysis: Decomposition of Total Effect into Direct, Indirect and Residual Effect: Risk Perception (y8) vs. 24 exogenous variables (x1-x24)

Residual effect: 0.529

Highest Indirect Individual effect: x_9 (13)

Result: Model 6.24 presents the path analysis by decomposing the total effect into direct, indirect and residual effects.

Revelation: It has been found that the variable **size of holding** has got both substantive direct and indirect effect on **risk perception.** When a farmer has larger size of holding, various types of risks for his enterprise also increases. More diversified land leads to their exposure towards more risk parameters. The exogenous variable **no. of female workers** has exerted the highest total effect. It implies that more involvement of female workers has more decisive effect on risks involved in the farm enterprise. It may be due to low level of education, low training exposure, among other reasons. The variable **size of holding** has rooted the highest indirect impact of as much as 13 exogenous variables to impact on the consequent variable y_8. In order to lower various risks, the FPO members must undertake proper planning to manage the land holding more effectively. The residual effect being **0.529**, it is to infer that even with the combination of 24 exogenous variables, **52.9 per cent variance** in y_8 (Risk perception) cannot be explained.

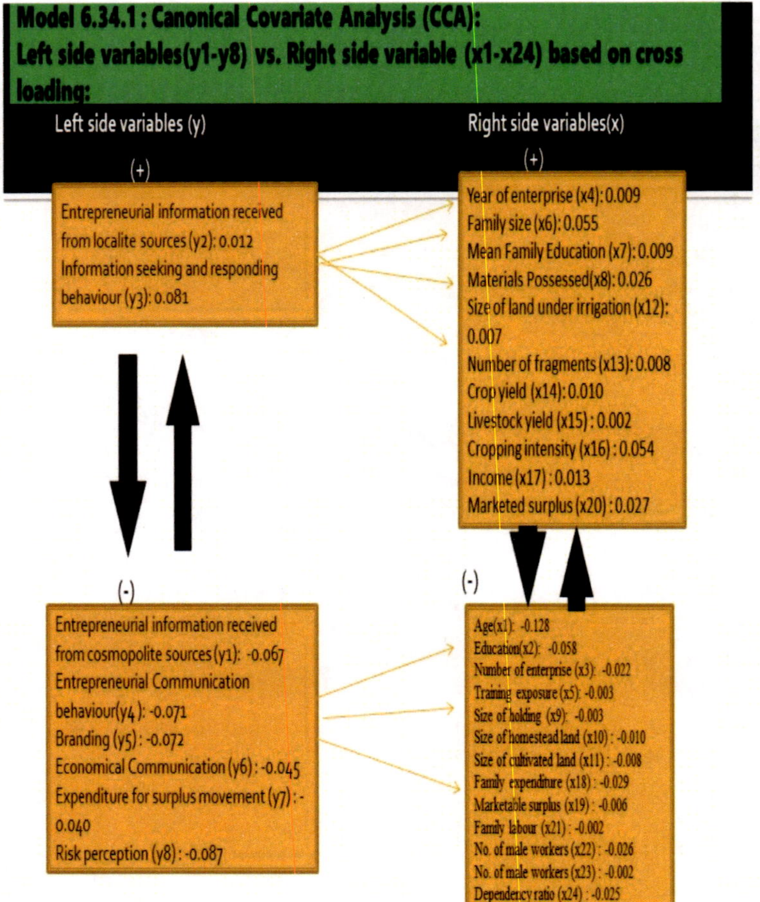

Model 6.25: Canonical Covariate Analysis: Interaction between left-side variables (y1-y8) and right-side variables (x1-x24) based on cross-loading:

Result: Canonical covariate analysis helps us understand and visualize the nature of sub-conglomeration between x and y variables.

Revelation: From the above illustrations it has been evinced that Entrepreneurial information received from localite sources (y_2) and Information seeking and responding behaviour (y_3) prefers to move together so it is well discernible that entrepreneurial information received from localite sources has developed intimate kinship with information seeking and responding behaviour.

When these two consequent variables are moving together, in one direction the right side variables year of enterprise (x_4), family size (x_6), mean family education (x_7), materials possessed (x_8), size of land under irrigation (x_{12}), number of fragments (x_{13}), crop yield (x_{14}), livestock yield (x_{15}), cropping intensity (x_{16}), income (x_{17}) and marketed surplus (x_{20}) selected and classified based on cross loading, are organically linked with the left side conglomeration of y variables.

Similarly, the following y variables have created a sub-conglomeration viz. entrepreneurial information received from cosmopolite sources (y_1), entrepreneurial communication behaviour (y_4), branding (y_5), economical communication (y_6), expenditure for surplus movement (y_7) and risk perception (y_8).

When this constellation of variables is interacting together, thus the following right side variables age (x_1), education (x_2), number of enterprise (x_3), training exposure (x5), size of holding (x9), size of homestead land (x10), size of cultivated land (x_{11}), family expenditure (x_{18}), marketable surplus (x_{19}), family labour (x_{21}), no. of male workers (x_{22}), no. of male workers (x_{23}) and dependency ratio (x_{24}) in a clandestine way have built up a close proximity with the right variables.

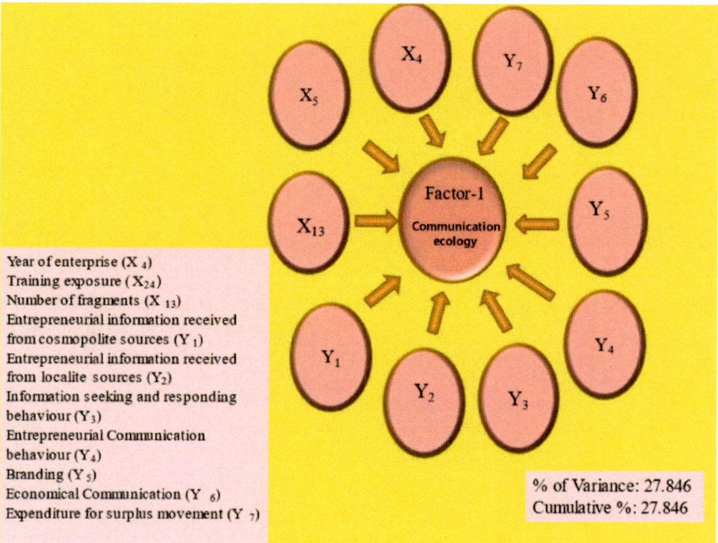

Model 6.26: Factor Analysis: Strategic Conglomeration of variables into Factor -1: Communication Ecology

Revelation: Accommodation of following year of enterprise (x_4), training exposure (x_{24}), number of fragments (x_{13}), entrepreneurial information received from cosmopolite sources (y_1), entrepreneurial information received from localite sources (y_2), information seeking and responding behaviour (y_3), entrepreneurial communication behaviour (y_4). branding (y_5), economical communication (y_6) and expenditure for surplus movement (y_7) has contributed 27.846 per cent of variance. This factor has been renamed as **"Communication ecology"**.

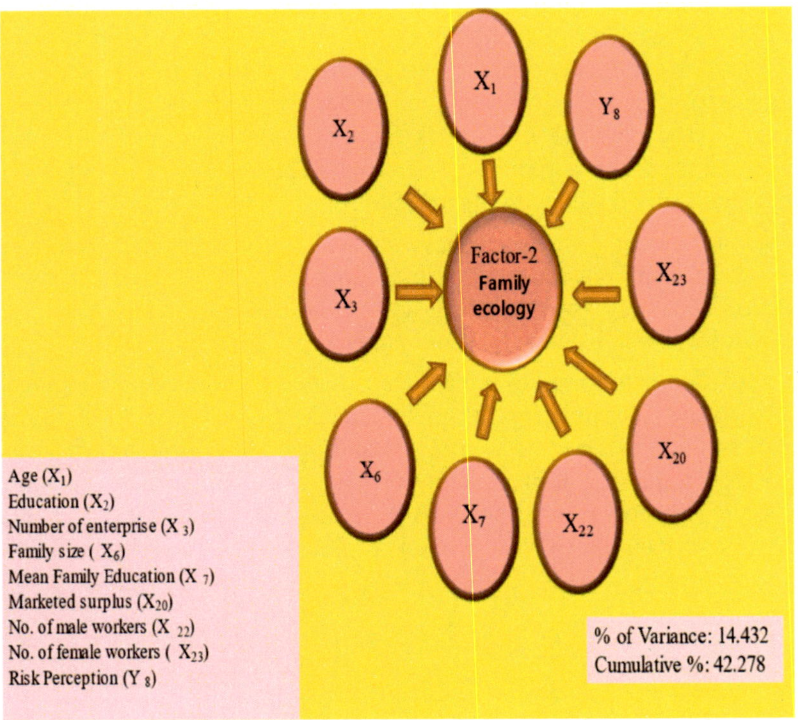

Model 6.27: Factor Analysis: Strategic Conglomeration of variables into Factor -2: Family Ecology

Revelation: Accommodation of following age (x_1),education (x_2), number of enterprise (x_3), family size (x_6), mean family education (x_7), marketed surplus (x_{20}), no. of male workers (x_{22}), no. of female workers (x_{23}) and risk perception (y_8)has contributed 14.432 per cent of variance. This factor has been renamed as **"Family ecology"**.

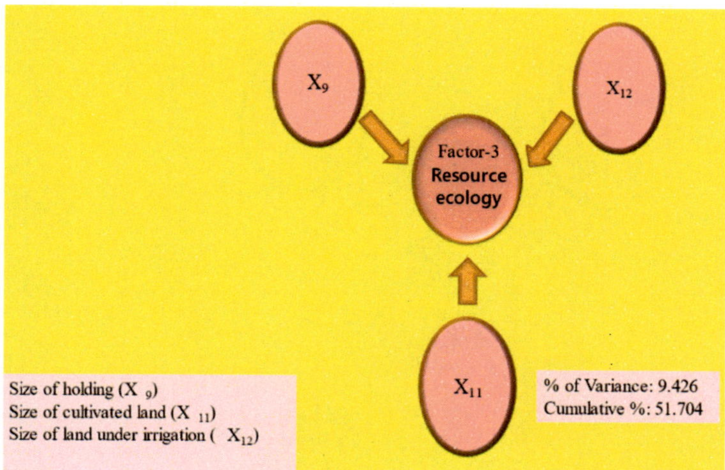

Model 6.28: Factor Analysis: Strategic Conglomeration of variables into Factor -3: Resource Ecology

Revelation: Accommodation of following size of holding (x_9), size of cultivated land (x_{11}) and size of land under irrigation (x_{12}) has contributed 9.426 per cent of variance. This factor has been renamed as **"Resource ecology"**.

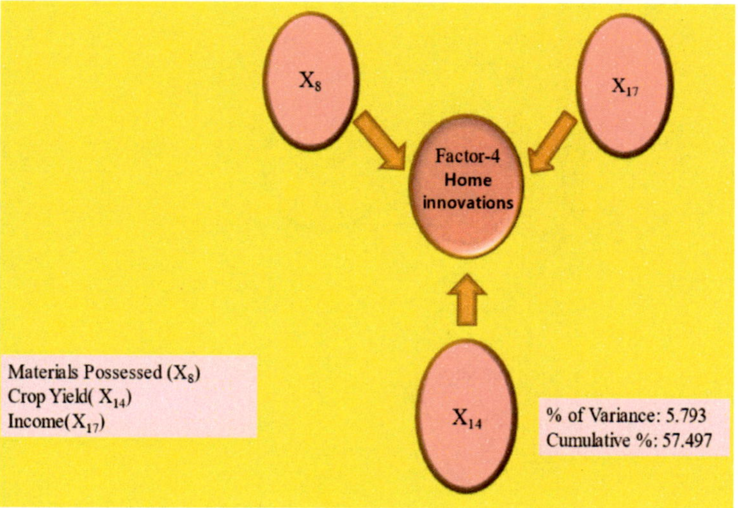

Model 6.29: Factor Analysis: Strategic Conglomeration of variables into Factor -4: Home Innovations

Revelation: Accommodation of following materials possessed (x_8), crop yield(x_{14}) and income(x_{17}) has contributed 5.793 per cent of variance. This factor has been renamed as **"Home innovations"**.

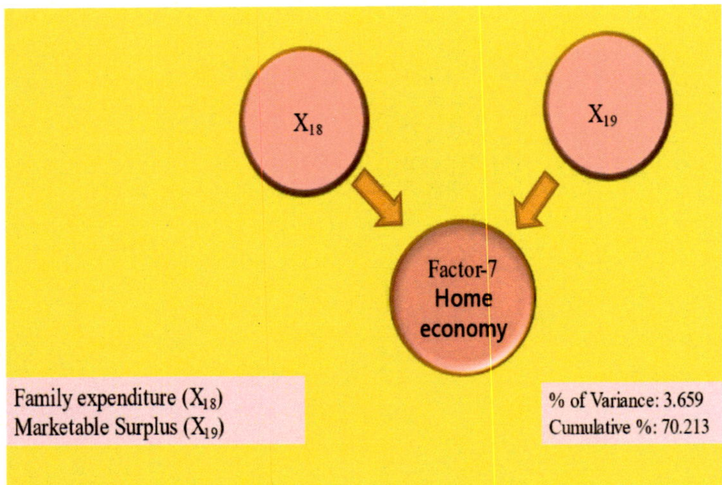

Model 6.30: Factor Analysis: Strategic Conglomeration of variables into Factor -7: Family Ecology

Revelation: Accommodation of following family expenditure (x_{18}) and marketable surplus (x_{19}) has contributed 3.659 per cent of variance. This factor has been renamed as "**Home economy**".

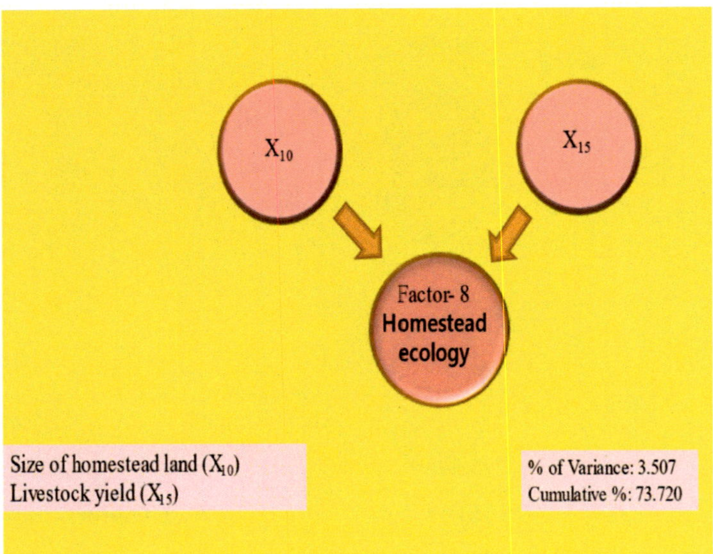

Model 6.31: Factor Analysis: Strategic Conglomeration of variables into Factor -8: Homestead Ecology

Revelation : Accommodation of following family expenditure (x_{18}) and marketable surplus (x_{19}) has contributed 3.507 per cent of variance. This factor has been renamed as "**Home economy**".

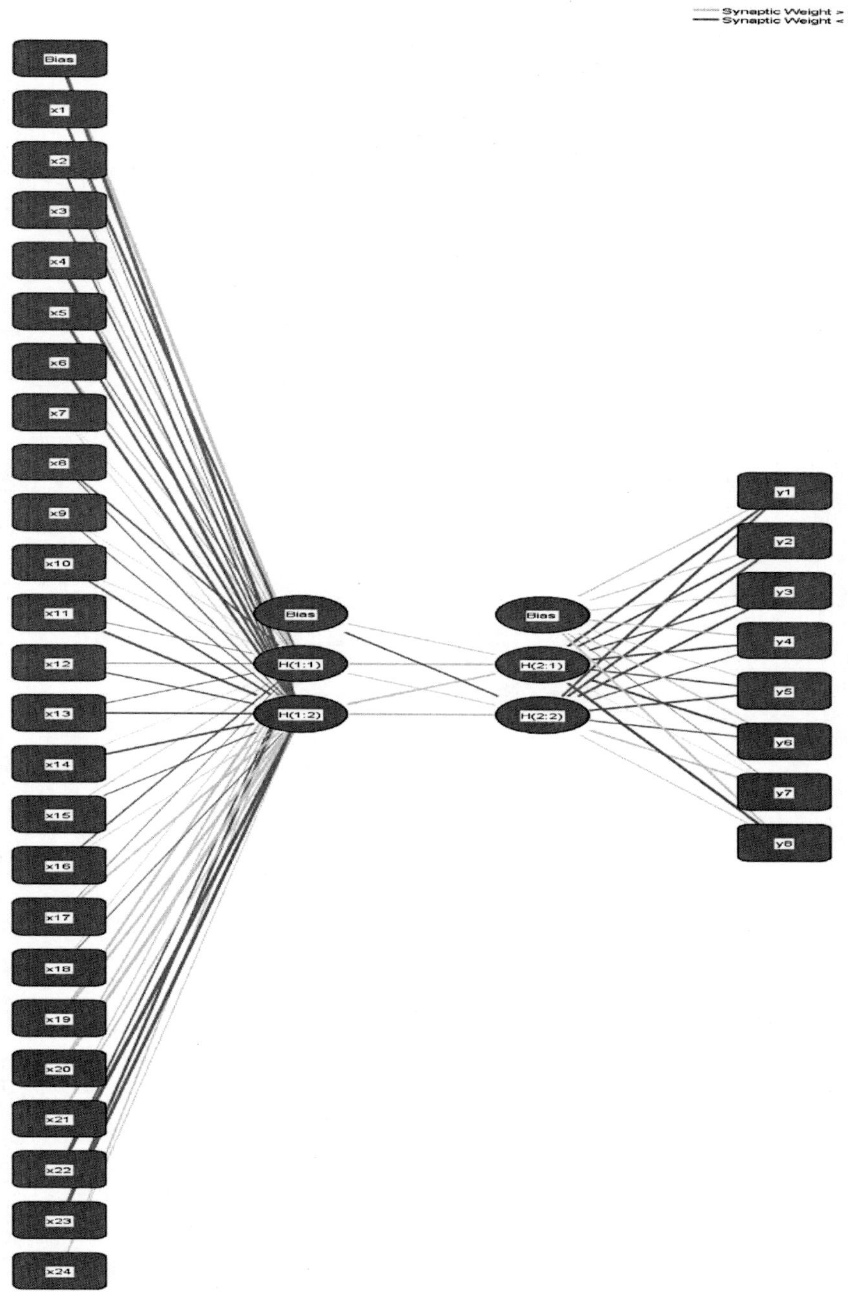

Model 6.32: Artificial Neural Networking

Model Summary			
Training	Sum of Squares Error		102.779
	Average Overall Relative Error		0.343
	Relative Error for Scale Dependents	Entrepreneurial info received from cosmopolite sources (y1)	0.201
		Entrepreneurial info received from localite sources (y2)	0.205
		Information seeking and responding behaviour (y3)	0.233
		Entrepreneurial communication behaviour (y4)	0.326
		Branding (y5)	0.234
		Economical communication (y6)	0.229
		Expenditure for surplus movement (y7)	0.575
		Risk perception (y8)	0.739
Testing	Sum of Squares Error		44.381
	Average Overall Relative Error		0.393
	Relative Error for Scale Dependents	Entrepreneurial info received from cosmopolite sources (y1)	0.336
		Entrepreneurial info received from localite sources (y2)	0.236
		Information seeking and responding behaviour (y3)	0.312
		Entrepreneurial communication behaviour (y4)	0.468
		Branding (y5)	0.382
		Economical communication (y6)	0.414
		Expenditure for surplus movement (y7)	0.917
		Risk perception (y8)	0.518

Revelation: Artificial Neural Network (ANN) has been carried out to measure the input variables (x1 – x24) passing through the hidden layers and ultimately impacting on the output variables (y1-y8).

Number of hidden layers depends on the number of errors are redressed for the training of input data. Hidden layers are made functional by adding bias to it to minimize the error. Now the following variables have exerted dominant impact on the output variables: Age (x1), Education (x2), Number of enterprise(x3), Year of enterprise (x4), Training exposure (x5), Family size (x6), No. of male workers (x22) and No. of female workers(x23).

So, these input variables have selected by applying ANN are of immense strategic implications and these variables merit special attention to deal with entrepreneurial behaviour of farmers in farmer producer organizations (FPO).

SWOT analysis of the FPOs under the study

A SWOT Analysis was performed with the help of a focus group discussion organised among the FPO members (Fig 6.1) with the following results :

Strength

- Block Agriculture Office and Block Horticulture Office are operating effectively.
- Presence of various other Line Departments.
- Strong Vegetable PG farmers support.
- Support from RMC and ORMAS.

Weakness

- Low and uncertain credit support credit Support.
- Lack of use of modern technology in farming.
- Poor irrigation source.

Opportunities

- Government support on subsidiary.
- Road transport.
- Climatic condition.
- Nearby Market : Bhubaneswar just 75km from Ranpur.

Threats

- Local Middleman.
- Inadequate supply of inputs in proper time.

Fig. 6.1: Focus group discussion with the FPO members at Village-Karadapalli

7

Conclusion

The present research had been conducted to study the Entrepreneurial behaviour of farmers in farmer producer organisations(FPO) in selected block of Odisha and in the end the comparison is made. The study had been conducted on 2 Farmer producer organisations (FPO) of Ranpur block from Nayagarh district of Odisha. A pilot study was conducted to understand the area,its people, institution ,communication and extension system of these states.

An exhaustive list of respondents was prepared critically with the help of FPO members. From the list, 100 respondents were selected for the study through Snowball sampling method. The primary data were collected with the help of structured interviewschedule by following the personal interview method. The secondary data werecollected from our departmental library, internet, Department ofAgriculture, Odisha, Bidhan Chandra Krishi Viswavidyalaya ,etc.for establishing the conceptual framework of the study.

The **general objective** of the study is to estimate and analyze the **Entrepreneurial behaviour of farmers in farmer producer organisations (FPO)** and the **specific objectives** are

- To estimate the level of entrepreneurial behaviour of farmers in FPO in terms of

  (i) Net return

  (ii) Marketable surplus

  (iii)Branding

  (iv)Entrepreneurial communication

- To estimate these 4 predicted characteristics of the enterprising farmers under FPO in terms of a set of socio-economic and managerial variables.
- To estimate the inter and intra level of interaction between sets of predicted and predictor variables as accommodated in the study.
- To generate policy at micro-level for farmers upskilling and upgradation of the entrepreneurial behaviour of study.
- To go for SWOT analysis of both farmers and FPOs to isolate the stronger and weaker points of enterprise ecology under study.

7.1. Summary

24 Independent variables and 8 Dependent variables were selected for the study respectively and measured with the help of exact scales developed by previous social science researchers or by modifying the developed scale by structured interview schedule for requirement of the study.

Independent variables selected for the study are, Age (x_1), Education (x_2), No. of enterprise (x_3), Year of enterprise (x_4), Training exposure (x_5), Family size (x_6), Mean Family education (x_7), Material possessed (x_8), Size of holding (x_9), Size of homestead land (x_{10}), Size of cultivated land (x_{11}), Size of land under irrigation (x_{12}), No. of fragments (x_{13}), Crop yield (x_{14}), Livestock yield (x_{15}), Cropping intensity (x16), Income (x_{17}), Family expenditure (x_{18}), Marketable surplus (x_{19}), Marketed surplus (x_{20}), Family labour (x_{21}), No. of male workers (x_{22}) No. of female workers (x_{23}) and dependency ratio (x_{24}). The Dependent variables selected for the study are Entrepreneurial info received from cosmopolite sources (y_1), Entrepreneurial info received from localite sources (y_2), Information seeking and responding behaviour (y_3), Entrepreneurial communication behaviour (y_4), Branding (y_5), Economical communication (y_6), Expenditure for surplus movement (y_7) and Risk perception (y_8).

The statistical tools viz., Mean, Median, Mode, Standard Deviation, Coefficient of variation, Correlation coefficient, Step wise Regression Analysis, Path analysis, Canonical covariate analysis, Factor Analysis and Artificial neural network were used for the purpose of the study.

Findings from the 2 FPOs of Ranpur Block from Nayagarh district of Odisha are given below

7.1.1 Coefficient of Correlation (r) between Entrepreneurial Information Received from Cosmopolite Sources (y_1) Vs. 24 Independent Variables

It has been found that the following variables age(x_1), number of enterprise (x_3), year of enterprise (x_4) training exposure (x_5), materials possessed (x_8), size of holding(x_9), size of cultivated land(x_{11}), size of land under irrigation (x_{12}), no. of fragments (x_{13}), crop yield (x_{14}), income (x_{17}), marketable surplus (x_{19}), marketed surplus (x_{20}), family labour (x_{21}), no. of male workers (x_{22}) and no. of female workers (x_{23}) recorded significant correlation with Entrepreneurial information received from cosmopolite sources (y_1).

7.1.2 Coefficient of Correlation (r) Between Entrepreneurial Information Received from Cosmopolite Sources (y_1) Vs. 24 Independent Variables

It has been found that the following variables age (x_1), education (x_2), no. of enterprise (x_3), year of enterprise (x_4), training exposure (x_5), family size (x_6), materials possessed (x_8), size of holding (x_9), size of cultivated land (x_{11}), size of land under irrigation (x_{12}), no. of fragments (x_{13}), crop yield (x_{14}), income (x_{17}), marketable surplus (x_{19}), marketed surplus (x_{20}), family labour (x_{21}), no. of male workers (x_{22}) and no. of female workers (x_{23}) recorded significant correlation with Entrepreneurial information received from localite sources (y_2).

7.1.3 Coefficient of Correlation (r) between Information Seeking and Responding Behaviour (y_3) and 24 Independent Variables

This presents the coefficient of correlation between Information seeking and Responding Behaviour (y_3) and 24 independent variables. It has been found age (x_1), education (x_2), no. of enterprise (x_3), year of enterprise (x_4), training exposure (x_5), family size (x_6), materials possessed (x8), size of holding (x_9), size of cultivated land (x_{11}), size of land under irrigation (x_{12}), no. of fragments (x_{13}), livestock yield (x_{15}), cropping intensity (x_{16}), marketable surplus (x_{19}), marketed surplus (x_{20}), no. of male workers (x_{22}) and no. of female workers (x_{23}) recorded significant correlation with Information seeking and Responding Behaviour (y_3).

7.1.4 Coefficient of Correlation (r) between Entrepreneurial Communication Behaviour(y_4) and 24 Independent Variables

It has been found that the following variables age (x_1), no. of enterprise (x_3), mean family education (x_7), materials possessed (x_8), size of holding (x_9), size of cultivated land (x_{11}), size of land under irrigation (x_{12}), no. of fragments (x_{13}), crop yield (x_{14}), livestock yield (x_{15}), marketable surplus (x_{19}), marketed surplus (x_{20}), no. of male workers (x_{22}) and no. of female workers (x_{23}) recorded significant correlation with Entrepreneurial communication behaviour(y_4).

7.1.5 Coefficient of Correlation (r) between Branding (y_5) and 24 Independent Variables

It has been found that the following variables age (x1), education (x_2), no. of enterprise (x_3), year of enterprise (x_4), training exposure (x_5), family size (x_6), materials possessed (x_8), size of holding (x_9), size of cultivated land (x_{11}), size of land under irrigation (x_{12}), no. of fragments (x_{13}), crop yield (x14), livestock yield (x_{15}), income (x_{17}), marketable surplus (x_{19}), marketed surplus (x_{20}), family labour (x_{21}), no. of male workers(x_{22}) and no. of female workers (x_{23}) recorded significant correlation with Economical Communication(y_5).

7.1.6 Coefficient of Correlation (r) between Economical communication (y_6) and 24 Independent Variables

This presents the coefficient of correlation between no. of enterprise (x_3), year of enterprise (x_4), mean family education (x_7), materials possessed (x_8), size of holding (x_9), size of cultivated land (x_{11}), size of land under irrigation (x_{12}), no. of fragments (x_{13}), crop yield (x_{14}), livestock yield (x_{15}), income (x_{17}), marketable surplus (x_{19}), marketed surplus (x_{20}), no. of male workers(x_{22}) and no. of female workers (x_{23}) recorded significant correlation with economical communication (y_6).

7.1.7 Coefficient of Correlation (r) between Expenditure for surplus Movement (y_7) and 24 Independent Variables

This presents the coefficient of correlation between age (x_1), education (x_2), no. of enterprise (x_3), year of enterprise (x4), training exposure (x_5), family size (x_6), materials possessed (x_8), cropping intensity (x_{16}), family expenditure (x_{18}), marketable surplus (x_{19}), marketed surplus (x_{20}) and family labour (x_{21}) recorded significant correlation with Transportation Cost (y_6). Number of enterprises (x_3), and Marketable surplus (x_{16}) recorded significant correlation with expenditure for surplus movement (y_7).

7.1.8 Coefficient of Correlation (r) between Risk Perception (y_8) and 24 Independent Variables

This presents the coefficient of correlation between age (x_1), education (x_2), no. of enterprise (x_3), year of enterprise (x_4), family size (x_6), size of land under irrigation (x_{12}), no. of male workers(x_{22}) and no. of female workers (x_{23}) recorded significant correlation with Transportation Cost (y_6).Number of enterprises (x_3), and Marketable surplus (x_{16}) recorded significant correlation with risk perception(y_8).

7.1.9 Stepwise Regression Analysis between Entrepreneurial Information Received from Cosmopolite sources (y_1) Vs. 24 Independent Variables

The six variables no. of fragments (x_{13}), crop yield (x_{14}), marketed surplus (x_{20}), no. of male workers(x_{22}), materials possessed (x_8), and training exposure (x_5) have been retained at the last step. The r^2 value being 68.70 %, these 6 variables have together contributed to 87.04 % of the total 71 % of explicated variables. the variables no. of fragments (x13), crop yield(x14), marketed surplus (x_{20}), no. of male workers(x_{22})materials possessed (x_8), and training exposure (x_5)were come up as strong determinants for the accessibility of entrepreneurial information from cosmopolite sources.

7.1.10 Stepwise Regression Analysis between Entrepreneurial information Received from Localite Sources (y_2) Vs. 24 Independent Variables

The five variables no. of male workers(x_{22}), no. of enterprise (x3), marketed surplus(x_{20}), size of land under irrigation (x_{12}) and crop yield (x_{14}) have been retained at the last step. The r^2 value being 61.80%. These five variables have together contributed to 87.04 % of the total 71.00% of explicated variables. The five variables no. of male workers(x_{22}), no. of enterprise (x3), marketed surplus(x_{20}), size of land under irrigation (x_{12}) and crop yield(x_{14}) were come up as strong determinants for the better accessibility of entrepreneurial information from localite sources.

7.1.11 Stepwise Regression Analysis between Information Seeking and Responding Behaviour (y_3) and 24 Causal Variables

The six variables no. of male workers (x_{22}), no. of enterprise (x_3), materials possessed (x_8), marketed surplus (x_{20}), Size of homestead land(x_{10}) and Size of cultivated land (x_{11}) have been retained at the last step. The r^2 value being 61.50%. These two variables have together contributed to 93.89 % of the total 65.50% of explicated variables. The six variables no. of male workers(x_{22}), no. of enterprise (x3), materials possessed (x_8), marketed surplus(x_{20}), Size of homestead land(x_{10}) and Size of cultivated land (x_{11}), were come up as strong determinants for accessibility to Information seeking and Responding Behaviour.

7.1.12 Stepwise Regression Analysis between Entrepreneurial Communication Behaviour (y_4) and 24 Causal Variables

The seven variables no. of male workers(x_{22}), materials possessed (x_8), marketed surplus (x_{20}), no. of fragments (x_{13}), crop yield (x_{14}), family labour (x_{21}) and Size of homestead land(x_{10}) have been retained at the last step. The r^2 value being 68.70%. These seven variables have together contributed to 95.15 % of the total 72.20% of explicated variables. The seven variables no. of male workers(x_{22}), materials possessed (x_8), marketed surplus (x_{20}), no. of fragments (x_{13}), crop yield (x14), family labour (x_{21}) and Size of homestead land(x_{10}) were come up as strong determinants for characterizing the entrepreneurial communication behaviour.

7.1.13 Stepwise Regression Analysis between Branding (y_5) and 24 Causal Variables

The six variables no. of male workers(x22),crop yield(x14),materials possessed (x8), training exposure(x5), no. of fragments (x13), Marketed surplus (x_{20}), have been retained at the last step. The r^2 value being 67.80%. These six variables have together contributed to 89.21% of the total 76 % of explicated variables. The six variables no. of male workers(x22),crop yield(x14),materials possessed (x_8), training exposure(x_5), no. of fragments (x_{13}), Marketed surplus (x_{20}),were come up as strong determinants for characterizing the Branding of agricultural products by FPO members.

7.1.14 Stepwise Regression Analysis between Economical Communication (y_6) and 24 Causal Variables :

The six variables no. of male workers($x_{22)}$, crop yield($x_{14)}$, materials possessed (x_8), no. of fragments (x_{13}), marketed surplus (x_{20}) and mean family education (x_7), have been retained at the last step. The r^2 value being 66.70%. These six variables have together contributed to 92% of the total 72.50% of explicated variables. The no. of male workers(x_{22}), crop yield(x14), materials possessed (x8), no. of fragments (x_{13}), marketed surplus (x_{20}) and mean family education (x_7), were come up as strong determinants for characterizing the economical communication undertaken by the FPO members.

7.1.15 Stepwise Regression Analysis between Expenditure for Surplus movement (y_7) and 24 Causal Variables

The four variables marketed surplus (x_{20}), training exposure(x_5),marketable surplus (x19) and cropping intensity(x_{16}) have been retained at the last step. The r^2 value being 68%. These four variables have together contributed to 95.63% of the total 71.10% of explicated variables. The four variables marketed surplus (x_{20}), training exposure(x_5), marketable surplus (x_{19}) and cropping intensity(x_{16}) were come up as strong determinants for characterizing the transportation cost of an enterprise.

7.1.16 Stepwise Regression Analysis between Risk Perception (y_8) and 24 Causal Variables

The four variables no. of female workers(x_{23}), year of enterprise (x_4), no. of enterprise (x_3) and crop yield(x_{14}) have been retained at the last step. The r^2 value being 37%. These two variables have together contributed to 78.38% of the total 47.20% of explicated variables. The four variables no. of female workers(x_{23}), year of enterprise (x_4), no. of enterprise (x_3) and crop yield(x_{14}) were come up as strong determinants for characterizing the transportation cost of an enterprise.

7.1.17 Path Analysis: Decomposition of Total Effect into Direct, Indirect and Residual Effect: Entrepreneurial information received from cosmopolite sources (y_1) Vs. 24 Independent Variables

While selecting potential entrepreneurs, they should be experienced. The variable size of holding (x_9) has routed the highest indirect effect of as many as thirteen(13) variables. So this variable is extremely important both for its highest direct effect as well as highest frequency of indirect effect .Here 27.40 % of exogenous variables can't explain this entrepreneurial information received from cosmopolite sources (y_1).

7.1.18 Path Analysis: Decomposition of Total Effect into Direct, Indirect and Residual Effect: Entrepreneurial Information Received from Localite sources(y_2) vs. 24 Exogenous Variables

The variable size of cultivated land (x_{11}) has routed the highest indirect effect of as many as twelve (12) variables. So this variable is extremely important both for its highest direct effect as well as highest frequency of indirect effect. Here 29% of exogenous variables can't explain this Entrepreneurial information received from localite sources (y_2).

7.1.19 Path Analysis: Decomposition of Total Effect into Direct, Indirect and Residual Effect: Information Seeking and Responding Behaviour (y_3) vs. 24 exogenous variables

The variable size of cultivated land (x_{11}) has routed the highest indirect effect of as many as fifteen (15) variables. So this variable is extremely important both for its highest direct effect as well as highest frequency of indirect effect. Here

34.50% of the total exogenous variables can't explain this Information seeking and responding behaviour (y_3).

7.1.20 Path Analysis: Decomposition of Total Effect into Direct, Indirect and Residual Effect: Entrepreneurial Communication Behaviour (y_4) vs. 24 exogenous Variables

The variable size of holding (x_9) has routed the highest indirect effect of as many as nine (9) variables. So this variable is extremely important both for its highest direct effect as well as highest frequency of indirect effect. Here 27.90% of the total exogenous variables can't explain this Entrepreneurial communication behaviour (y_4).

7.1.21 Path Analysis: Decomposition of Total Effect into Direct, Indirect and Residual Effect: Branding (y_5) vs. 24 Exogenous Variables

The variable training exposure (x_5) has routed the highest indirect effect of as many as eleven (11) variables. The highest direct effect is exerted by no. of male workers and is important for branding. Here 24.10% of the total exogenous variables can't explain this branding (y_5).

7.1.22 Path Analysis: Decomposition of Total Effect into Direct, Indirect and Residual Effect: Economical Communication (y_6) vs. 24 Exogenous variables

The variable size of holding (x_9) has routed the highest indirect effect of as many as ten (10) variables. So this variable is extremely important both for its highest direct effect as well as highest frequency of indirect effect. Here 27.70% of the total exogenous variables can't explain this economical communication (y_6).

7.1.23 Path Analysis: Decomposition of Total Effect into Direct, Indirect and Residual Effect: Expenditure for Surplus Movement (y_7) vs. 24 Exogenous Variables

The variable marketed surplus (x_{20}) has routed the highest indirect effect of as many as thirteen (13) variables. So this variable is extremely important both for its highest direct effect as well as highest frequency of indirect effect. Here 29% of the total exogenous variables can't explain this expenditure for surplus movement (y_7).

7.1.24 Path Analysis: Decomposition of Total Effect into Direct, Indirect and Residual Effect: Risk Perception (y_8) vs. 24 Exogenous Variables

The variable size of holding (x_9) has routed the highest indirect effect of as many as thirteen (13) variables. So this variable is extremely important both for its highest direct effect as well as highest frequency of indirect effect. Here 52.90% of the total exogenous variables can't explain this risk perception (y_8).

7.1.25 Canonical Covariate Analysis: Interaction between Left Side Dependent and Right Side Independent Variables Based on Cross-loading

It has been evinced that Entrepreneurial information received from localite sources (y_2) and Information seeking and responding behaviour (y_3) prefers to move together so it is well discernible that entrepreneurial information received from localite sources has developed intimate kinship with information seeking and responding behaviour.

When these two consequent variables are moving together, in one direction the right side variables year of enterprise (x_4), family size (x_6), mean family education (x_7), materials possessed (x_8), size of land under irrigation (x_{12}), number of fragments (x_{13}), crop yield (x_{14}), livestock yield (x_{15}), cropping intensity (x_{16}), income (x_{17}) and marketed surplus (x_{20}) selected and classified based on cross loading, are organically linked with the left side conglomeration of y variables.

Similarly, the following y variables have created a sub-conglomeration viz. entrepreneurial information received from cosmopolite sources (y1), entrepreneurial communication behaviour (y4), branding (y_5), economical communication (y_6), expenditure for surplus movement (y_7) and risk perception (y_8).

When this constellation of variables is interacting together, thus the following right side variables age (x_1), education (x_2), number of enterprise (x_3), training exposure (x_5), size of holding (x9), size of homestead land (x_{10}), size of cultivated land (x_{11}), family expenditure (x_{18}), marketable surplus (x_{19}), family labour (x_{21}), no. of male workers (x_{22}), no. of male workers (x_{23}) and dependency ratio (x_{24}) in a clandestine way have built up a close proximity with the right variables.

7.1.26 Factor Analysis by Conglomeration of 24 Independent Variables (x1to x24) of 2 Farmer Producer Organisations of Ranpur block from Nayagarh District of Odisha. into 6 Factors, Based on Factor Loading and Renaming of all the Factors

Factor analysis is a data reduction approach. Here the total number of interacting variable, based on factor loading and Eigen values, has been grouped into identifiable factor. Each factor is retaining the homogeneous variable, strongly bound to each other towards taking a strategic decision for effective management of resource or organization.

It has been found that,

Factor 1 has accommodated the following variables viz. year of enterprise (x_4), training exposure (x_{24}), number of fragments (x_{13}), entrepreneurial information received from cosmopolite sources (y_1), entrepreneurial information received from localite sources (y_2), information seeking and responding behaviour (y_3), entrepreneurial communication behaviour (y_4), branding (y_5), economical communication (y_6) and expenditure for surplus movement (y_7) has contributed 27.846 per cent alone and 27.846 per cent cumulatively to explain the variance. This factor has been renamed as "**Communication ecology**".

Factor 2 has accommodated the following variables, viz. age (x_1), education (x_2), number of enterprise (x_3), family size (x_6), mean family education (x_7), marketed surplus (x_{20}), no. of male workers (x_{22}), no. of female workers (x_{23}) and risk perception (y_8) has contributed 14.432 per cent alone and 42.278 per cent cumulatively to explain the variance. This factor has been renamed as "**Family ecology**".

Factor 3 has accommodated the following variables, viz. size of holding (x_9), size of cultivated land (x_{11}) and size of land under irrigation (x_{12}) has contributed 9.426 per cent alone and 51.704 per cent cumulatively to explain the variance. This factor has been renamed as "**Resource ecology**".

Factor 4 has accommodated the following variables, viz., materials possessed (x_8), crop yield(x_{14}) and income(x_{17}) has contributed 5.793 per cent alone and 57.497 per centcumulatively to explain the variance. This factor has been renamed as "**Home innovations**".

Factor 5 has accommodated the following variables, viz., Family labour (x_{21}) and has not been renamed because it consists of single variable. There is no need of categorization. It has contributed to 4.885 per cent alone and 62.381 per cent cumulatively to explain the variance.

Factor 6 has accommodated the following variables, viz., Cropping intensity (x_{16}) and has not been renamed because it consists of single variable. It has contributed to 4.172 per cent alone and 66.554 per cent cumulatively to explain the variance.

Factor 7 has accommodated the following variables, viz., family expenditure (x_{18}) and marketable surplus (x_{19}) has contributed 3.659 per cent alone and 70.213 per centcumulatively to explain the variance. This factor has been renamed as "**Home economy**".

Factor8 has accommodated the following variables, viz,,size of homestead land (x_{10}), livestock yield(x_{15}) has contributed 3.507 per cent alone and 73.720 per centcumulatively to explain the variance. This factor has been renamed as "**Homestead ecology**".

Factor9 has accommodated the following variable, viz., dependency ratio (x_{24}) and has not been renamed because it consists of single variable. It has contributed to 3.325 per cent alone and 77.045 per cent cumulatively to explain the variance.

7.1.27 Artificial Neural Network

Artificial Neural Network (ANN) has been carried out to measure the input variables ($x_1 - x_{24}$) passing through the hidden layers and ultimately impacting on the output variables (y_1-y_8).

Number of hidden layers depends on the amount of errors are redressed for the training of input data. Hidden layers are made functional by adding bias to it to minimize the error. Now the following variables have exerted dominant impact on the output variables : Age (x_1), Education (x_2) Number of enterprise(x_3), Year of enterprise (x_4), Training exposure (x_5), Family size (x_6),No. of male workers(x_{22}) and No. of female workers(x_{23}).

So, these input variables have selected by applying ANN are of immense strategic implications and these variables merit special attention to deal with entrepreneurial behaviour of farmers in farmer producer organisations (FPO).

7.2 Recommendations

Based on the empirical research, following recommendations can be made for this specific area of research

- Land size based planning for business communication can help the growth and success of farm enterprise.
- Social capitals like, Schools, Panchayats, Credit organizations, market-linked institutions, are to be integrated for shaping up a new form of Entrepreneurial communication behaviour.
- Hassle-free Credit facilities to be provided to the FPO members to avoid the issue of red-tapism which will save time and resources of the farmers.
- Integrated Storage facilities to be created to preserve the surplus produce of the farmers and avoid wastage of farm produce.
- Training, focusing on business communication, handling ICT tools and mobile telephony, can go along way for making communication behaviour more adaptive to present social ecology of agriculture and allied sectors of Odisha.
- Land fragmentation has to be minimized to optimize the use of resources available with the farmers.
- The size of land under irrigation has to be increased to increase the marketed surplus which will improve the farmers' economic condition.
- Branding of products to be done to provide importance to the local products and maintain the unique identity of the produce.
- Proper information regarding the condition of farm ecology is to be provided to the farmers to manage the farms in a better way.

7.3 Limitations of the Research

The most important limitations which have beenobservedin this research are as follows:

- Bench marking on the status of reigning of 'Entrepreneurial communication' has really been a difficult task.
- Number of respondents could have been more.
- The study should have been done in different locations and different times.

- There were problems of overlapping of some variables that could have been avoided.
- Some new scales could have been better if created.
- Since the concept is complex, it was very difficult to get qualitative response.
- Nowadays, farmers have become very profession oriented and hesitate to interact and generate information without expectation. That created barriers sometimes to get relevant information unleashed of them.

7.4 Future Scope of the Research

The current study was carried out by delving further into the type, severity, and character of the challenges that are impeding entrepreneurial communication. Entrepreneurial communication is now a need in these days of unemployment and stands to be both the means and technique of maintaining life processes in terms of both assets and capital; nonetheless, it requires more extensive research. Developing entrepreneurial communication among aspiring and motivated entrepreneurs anywhere is a never-ending activity in and of itself. As a result, the current study leaves the following domains to be explored further in the future:

1) More research can be done to model entrepreneurial communication, particularly positive motivation.
2) Future research on this issue may incorporate numerous contextual and realistic elements in addition to those included in this study.
3) Further research on a comparable issue will help you understand the structure and function of entrepreneurial communication behaviour and process.
4) There is room for methodological innovation in the future, as well as the use of artificial intelligence in this study.
5) Policy study on entrepreneurship and entrepreneurial communication in order to monitor or rationalise the volume of rural entrepreneurship in order to maintain the rate of expansion uninterrupted.
6) In agricultural marketing and rural development research, social networking, business communication, co-integrating communication behaviour with market analysis, and data analytics may go a long way toward generating alternative and scenario analysis.
7) Gender problems can be used more extensively in future research on this topic.
8) Empirical researchers are required to assess the worth of economic and ecological losses caused by the system's entrepreneurial behaviour.

7.5. Conclusion

The entire study elicits the following conclusions remarks to make –

1. FPO is the future pathway for Indian farmers to earn both income and food security.
2. Eight echelons of FPOs {Entrepreneurial information received from cosmopolite sources(y_1) Entrepreneurial information received from localite sources (y_2), information seeking and responding behaviour (y_3), Entrepreneurial communication behaviour (y_4), branding (y_5), Economical communication (y_6), Expenditure for surplus movement (y_7) and Risk Perception (y_8)} have been selected to examine and elucidate their interactive nature which are related with the growth and prospects of FPOs.
3. Some of the following operating variables have been found to discharge strong functional impact on entrepreneurial behaviour of farmers in FPO : Number of fragments (x_{13}), Crop yield (x_{14}), no. Of male workers (x_{22}), Marketed surplus (x_{20}), Materials possessed (x_8), Training exposure (x_5).
4. The following factors have been extracted by applying PCA viz., Communication ecology, Family ecology, resource ecology, home innovations, home economy and homestead ecology. These factors have got tremendous strategic and policy implications.

Conclusively, it has been observed that in Odisha, the level of entrepreneurial growth in agriculture at a certain sustainable level and scope to improve more. More number of variables have been found positively and significantly correlated to determine the elevation of entrepreneurial communication. However, the study has got tremendous policy implication, a part of which is uniquely suitable for Odisha's social ecology.

Bibliography

Abeyrathne, H.R.M.P. & Jayawardena, L.N.A.C.(2014). Impact of group interactions on farmers' entrepreneurial behaviour. Ekonomie and Management. 17:46-57.

Acharya, S.K. & Roy, S. (2021). Entrepreneurial Communication in Agriculture.

Ahuja, Rakesh., Singh, S., Sangwan, S.S. & Gautam.(2021). Entrepreneurial behaviour of dairy farmers in haryana.

Amitha, C., Savitha, B., Sudha Rani, V. & Laxminarayana, P. (2021). Farmer Producer Organizations (FPOs) – Analysis of Profile of FPOs and Its Members in Medak District of Telangana. Current J. App. Sci. and Tech. 24-31.

Battu, P., Acharya, S.K., Kanagaraj, M. & Haque, M. (2022). Entrepreneurial behaviour of Self Help Groups: Enterprise, Income and Efficiency. J. of Comm. Mobil. and Sust. Devt. 17(1) :329-332.

Bhatt, R.S., (1974). Growth of entrepreneurship in small and medium sectors. The Indian J. Pub Admini. 20(3) :453-465.

Calder, L.M., and Ross, F. (1976). Group organisation and leadership in rural life. Lucas Bros, Columbia, Missouri.

Cole, A.H. (1968). Meso-economics: A contribution from entrepreneurial history. Explorations in Entrepreneurial History. 6(1): 78-86.

Darling, J. R., & Beebe, S. A. (2007). Effective entrepreneurial communication in organization development: Achieving excellence based on leadership strategies and values. Org Devt J. 25(1): 76.

Datta, J., Das, J. & Dilip Kumar, R. (2016). Entrepreneurial behaviour of rural women in Tripura.

De, D. (1986). Factors affecting entrepreneur characteristics of farmers. Indian J. Soc Work. 541-546.

Dechamma, S., Bommaiah, K. & Shanabhoga, M.B. (2022). Attitude of Farmer Producer Organizations Members Towards the Organization development. Vikas Publishing House Pvt. Ltd., New Delhi, pp. 46-92.

Desai, V. (1999). Entrepreneurship and Technology. Himalaya Publishing House, Mumbai,

Dey, A., Gautam, Y. & Sharma, A. (2022). Assessment of Marketable Surplus of Rice and Wheat in Rohatas District of Bihar. 67. 289-295.

Dhineshwari, S., Selvam, S., Amarnath, S. & Prabakaran, K. (2021). Performance Analysis of the Farmer Producer Companies in Western Tamil Nadu, India using Altman's Z-score. Madras Agril J. 108.

Fisher, D.A. (1982). The myopia of learning. Strategic Mgmt. J .14:95-112

Fraser, T.M. (1961). Achievement motivation as a factor in rural development, a report on research in Western Orissa. Haverford College, Haverford, Paris.

Gregoric, M., Haleuš, J., Zeman, S. & Vovk, A. (2018). The importance of branding of agricultural products with quality labels and their recognition in croatian market.

Gurjar, R. & Verma, J. (2022). Entrepreneurial Behaviour of Beekeeping Farmers. p 42

Hagen, G.C. (1962). The relevance of psychology to the explanation of social phenomena. Borger, R., Cioffi, F. (Ed.). Explanation in the behavioural sciences. Cambridge University Press, Cambridge, pp. 313-326.

Harikrishna, Y., Hansdah, P. & Sharma, N. (2022). Farmer's Producer Organisation (FPO) – Collective Steps towards Lucrative Agriculture. Asian J. Agril. Ext., Econ & Socio. 60-65.

Harper, M., and Vyakaranam, S. (1988). Rural enterprise: Case studies for developing countries. Intermediate technology publications, London.

Jamir, T. & Jha, K. (2020). Entrepreneurial Behaviour of King Chilli Growers in Peren District, Nagaland. Internat. J. Current Microb. Appl. Sci. 9.

Jha, K.K. (2012). Entrepreneurial behaviour of pineapple growers. Indian Res. J. Extn Edn.1:142-145.

Jha, K.K. (2012). Factors influencing entrepreneurial behaviour of potato growers. J. of Interacademicia. 16:1023-1028.

Kacharu, T. A. (2013). Entrepreneurial Behaviour of floriculturist. M.Sc. (Ag.) Thesis. Dr. Punjab Rao Deshmukh Krishi Vidyapeeth, Akola, Maharashtra, India. 144p.

Kumar, P., Perumal, A., Kar, A., Jha, G. & Rao, D. (2018). Progress and Performance of States in Promotion of Farmer Producer Organisations in India. 54:108-113.

Lakshmi, S., Jaya, G. & Gummagolmath, K. (2021). SWOT Analysis of Farmers' Perceptions on Farmer Producer Companies: A Study in Maharashtra, India. Curr. J. Appl. Sci.Tech. 124-135.

Leagans, J.P., (1961). The future of entrepreneurial research. Explorations in entrepreneurial history. Second series, Vol (1), pp. 3-9.

Li, Q., Zhang, L., Chen, Y., Shao, S., Wang, T., Tian, H., Shi, Y. & Wang, S. (2021). Research on the Influence of Farmers' Entrepreneurial Motivation on Entrepreneurial Performance.

Madhumitha, S., Chandrasekaran, K., Kumar, R. & Selvi, R. (2020). Determinants of Entrepreneurial Behaviour of Women Agripreneurs in Namakkal District. Internat. J. of Curr. Microb. Appl. Sci. 9. 1428-1435.

Manaswi, H., Kumar, P., Kar, A., Perumal, A., Jha, G., Rao, M. & Prakash, P. (2019). Impact of Farmer Producer Organisations on organic chilli (Capsicum frutescens) production in Telangana. Indian J. Agril. Sci. 89.

Manjula, S. (1995). A study of entrepreneurial behaviour of rural women in Ranga Reddy district of Andhra Pradesh. M. Sc. (Home Science). Thesis, ANGRAU, Rajendra Nagar, Hyderabad

Mc clelland, D.C. (1961). Motivating economic achievement. Free Press, New York.

Mc clelland, D.C. (1965). Need achievement and entrepreneurship: a longitudinal study. J. Persona. Soc. Psych. (1):389-392.

Minten, B., Singh, K. & Sutradhar, R. (2013). Branding and agricultural value chains in developing countries: Insights from Bihar (India). Food Policy. 38. 23-34.

Mubarak, A., Irham, I., Mulyo, J. & Hartono, S. (2019). The influence of entrepreneurship characteristics and competencies on farmers' entrepreneurial intentions in the border region of North Borneo. IOP Conference Series: Earth and Environmental Science.

Narayanan, S. (2021). Marketable Surplus of Banana in Dindigul District of Tamil Nadu. J. Entrepr. Org. Mgmtt. 10. 1-5.

Naveen, K. P. (2012). Entrepreneurial Behaviour of pomegranate farmers of Chitradurga district of Karnataka. M.Sc. (Ag.) Thesis. University of Agricultural Science, Bangalore. India. 164p.

Neill, R.E., and Rogers, E.M. (1963). Measuring achievement motivation among farmers. Department series A.E. 3446. Ohio Agricul. Expt. Stn. Columbus.

Nwachukwu, D., & Nwadighoha.(2022). E. E. Agripreneurship Marketing and Economic Recovery in Post COVID-19 Era in Ikwerre LGA in Rivers State.

Nwaiwu, I. & Onyeagocha, S. (2021). Determinants of net returns from garden egg.

Ommani, A. (2011). Strengths, weaknesses, opportunities and threats (SWOT) analysis for farming system businesses management: Case of wheat farmers of Shadervan District, Shoushtar Township, Iran. Afr. J. Bus. Manag. 5.

Paladan, N. (2021). Developing Farmers and Fisherfolks Entrepreneurial Capacity towards Community Based-Enterprise. 05. 105-115.

Palanivelu, A., and Rajanarayanam, S. (2005). Definition of Entrepreneurs in new millennium. Kisan World. 32(6):28-31.

Patel, M.M., and Sanoria, Y.C. (1997). Correlates of entrepreneurial behaviour of sugarcane growers. Maharashtra J. Extn. Edn. Vol. (16), pp. 344-346.

Plastina, A., Liu, F., Sawadgo, W., Miguez, F., Carlson, S. & Marcillo, G. (2018). Annual Net Returns to Cover Crops in Iowa. J. Appl. Farm Econ. 2. 10.7771/2331-9151.1030.

Pongener, S. & Jha, K.K. (2020). Entrepreneurial behaviour of off season cucumber growers: an analysis. Plant Archives. 20. 763-768.

Prasad, D., Lakhera, J., Tyagi, S., Sharma, D. & Kumar, S. (2021). Entrepreneurial Behaviour of Dairy Farmers in North-Western Rajasthan. International J. Curr. Microb. Appl. Sci. 10.

Prashad, A. (1988). Entrepreneurship development under TRYSEM. Concept Publicity Company, New Delhi.

Rao, G.K.V. (1985). A prediction analysis of farming performance of farmers through their entrepreneurial behavior factors. Ph.D. thesis, A.P.A.U. Rajendra Nagar, Hyderabad.

Rao, T.V., and Mehta, P. (1978). Psychological Factors in Entrepreneurship.

Rath, S., Sahoo, P. & Sarangi, K. (2021). Farmer Producer Organisations: Effective Tool for Coping with the COVID-19 Crisis.

Reddy, A.A. (2021). Scaling up of Farmer Producer Organizations in India. Academia Letters.

Roy, D., Sonkar, V., Singh, R.K.P. & Kumar, A. (2020). Comparative Study of Farmer Producer Organizations in Bihar and Maharashtra.

Sachitra, V. (2020). An Examination of Cinnamon Farmers Entrepreneurial Behaviour in Sri Lankan Context. 153-176.

Schumpter, J.A. (1970). The entrepreneur as innovator. Reading in management (second edition). Mc Graw Hill, New York. Schwartz, E.A. (1979). Entrepreneurship: New female frontier. J Contemp. Busi. Winter Issue.15:150-163.

Sharma, P., Upreti, H., Ojha, K. & Gupta, S. (2019). Role of Government, Private and Cooperative Stakeholders in Development and promotion of Financial Products: A Study of Farmers Producers Organisations (FPOs). Internat. J. Innov. Tech Explo. Engi. 8. 19-28.

Shirur, M., Chandregowda, J., Shivalingegowda, S. & Rana, Rajesh. (2017). Entrepreneurial behaviour and socio economic analysis of mushroom growers in Karnataka. Indian J. Agril Sci. 87. 840-845.

Siddaiah, R. (2021). International Journal of Agriculture and Plant Science Online A study on net returns from various sources and incremental net returns to the farmers of cauvery command areas: An Economic Analysis. Internat J. Pest Mgmt.

Singh, M., Tiwari, D. & Dhillon, G. (2021). Attitude of the Farmers towards Farmer Producer Organisations (FPOs) in Punjab.

Singh, M., Tiwari, D., & Rana, R. (2022). Role of Organizational Structure and Behaviour for Ensuring Sustainability of Farmer Producer Organisations in Punjab. J. Krishi Vigyan. 10.

Singh, M., Tiwari, D., Monga, S. & Rana, R. (2022). Behavioural Determinants of Functionality of Farmer Producer Organisations in Punjab. Indian J. of Extn Educn. 58(1):130-135

Singh, P. N. (1986). Factors influencing entrepreneurship. Developing entrepreneur-ship for economic development. Vikas Publishing House Pvt. Ltd., New Delhi, pp. 46-92.

Singh, S. (2021). Producer Companies as New Generation Cooperatives. Economic and Political Weekly. 43: 22-24.

Sun, Y., Huang, Y., Fang, X., Yan, F. (2022). The Purchase Intention for Agricultural Products of Regional Public Brands: Examining the Influences of Awareness, Perceived Quality, and Brand Trust. Mathematical Problems in Engineering. 2022. 1-10.

Suryawanshi, O.P. (2018). Enhancement of market price of rice by value addition and entrepreneurship. Internat. J. Agric. Engg., 11(Sp. Issue) : 105-109.

Swamy, B.A. (1988). Agricultural entrepreneurship in India. Ph.D. Thesis, Andhra University, Waltair, Andhra Pradesh.

Tiwari, N., Syed, H. & Mazhar. (2022). Entrepreneurial behaviour of rose growers in prayagraj district of uttar Pradesh . Internat J. of Nat. and App Scs. 11: 53-58.

U. (Eds.). Developing entrepreneurship. A hand book of Learning systems, New Delhi.

Uzelac, O., Dukić M., Marijana. & Lukinovic, M. (2022). The role of branding agricultural products in better market valorization. Ekonomika Poljoprivrede. 69: 613-625.

Zhang, Z., Zhao, H. & Zeng, X. (2021). Government subsidies and online branding for agricultural products. Evolutionary Intelligence.

Websites Accessed During Study and Referred

https://www.fpoodisha.nic.in/

https://www.researchgate.net

https://www.google.co.in/imghp?hl=en&ogbl

https://www.nayagarh.nic.in

http://odihort.nic.in/agriculturepolicy